Called
to
Live

Called to Live

A Chronicle of
Recovery After
Attempted Suicide

Nancy Virden

TATE PUBLISHING
AND ENTERPRISES, LLC

Published by Tate Publishing & Enterprises, LLC
127 E. Trade Center Terrace | Mustang, Oklahoma 73064 USA
1.888.361.9473 | www.tatepublishing.com

Tate Publishing is committed to excellence in the publishing industry. The company reflects the philosophy established by the founders, based on Psalm 68:11,
"The Lord gave the word and great was the company of those who published it."

Book design copyright © 2013 by Tate Publishing, LLC. All rights reserved.
Cover design by Lauro Talibong
Interior design by Jomel Pepito

Published in the United States of America

ISBN: 978-1-62295-334-9
1. Biography & Autobiography / Personal Memoirs
2. Biography & Autobiography / Medical
12.11.26

DEDICATION

This book is dedicated to all individuals facing the daily storm of mental illness publicly with their heads held high, defying forceful winds of stigma and ignorance. It is you I admire, you who inspire me, and it is you who will change the world.

Acknowledgements

From the very beginning, it has mostly been the encouragement of two people whose belief in the book's potential, and enthusiasm for my writing, has inspired movement toward pursuing this goal. *If it were not for you two, I doubt this book would exist. Jerry Virden,* you watered the seed of an idea, giving it the strength to sprout with the words, "That is why it is so important for you to write." Your continued support and patience have been invaluable. You read my rough draft and offered valuable insight; your openness to public exposure of our marriage is a treasure indeed. Thank you for the heart behind all of these generous gifts. *Dr. Jason Baruti,* you nurtured the budding plant by prompting me to write for your clients and by calling my writing "inspiring." Thank you for offering the means to chănging my worldview or there would nothing to write.

Thank you also to the following:

Jonathan and Timothy Virden, your love has been the undergirding of my recovery even though for the longest time you were not aware there was a crisis. Throughout my recovery, God gave each of you wise and timely words to help change my thinking for the positive. I know you believe in me and are proud of your mom. The feeling is mutual.

Lynne Cannenta, you faithfully present an optional, healthier point of view, steering me toward clearer thinking. Your reassurance has been invaluable many times over.

Every one of you group members who have walked portions of this journey with me have benefitted me with your wisdom and input. I pray you are doing well.

To all of the above, and to Tate Publishing for taking a chance on me, are extended countless hearty and sincere thanks. I long for a more accurate way of expressing how deeply appreciative I feel.

TABLE OF CONTENTS

DEAD

"I won't drink it."

A young surgical resident had been using all his persuasive powers to convince me to swallow a dish-soap flavored liquid. "This test is important for you to be well," he had been insisting for nearly fifteen minutes.

"Now why would I care about that? I will not drink it. It tastes nasty."

Frustrated, he pulled out a new tactic. "All these people here in this room cannot go home until you take this test. Their shift ends at eleven o'clock, and as long as you resist they will have to stay and be unable to go home to their families."

It was nearly eleven p.m. If not for the fact that the young woman serving as my suicide watch-guard had already mentioned her shift ended at that hour, dismissing his ploy would have been easy. He had stirred the one thing I did still care about, not wanting to make someone else's life miserable. To continue stubbornly refusing medical treatment could possibly keep these techs and nurses from going home. What if that were true?

Looking the radiologist in the eye, I inquired whether she would be one who had to stay.

"No," she replied keeping intense eye contact. "But I am the only radiologist on this shift qualified to read films. As long as I am with you other patients will have to wait."

"So, go help the other people."

"I'm not allowed to leave you."

A few minutes later, picturing the halls lined with groaning patients who could not get medical help because of me, I grudgingly agreed to take the test that could potentially save my life.

•• • ••

Major Depression had been hammering away for months at any reasons I may have held for living. In one final blow, it had managed to convince me God wanted me to give up. As a committed Christian, I did not want to disobey my Heavenly Father. His permission for suicide was necessary. I asked him, "Please, God. Is it time?"

The reply was not God's voice. My fractured mind said, "Yes, it's okay. Come home." Peace came over me, and tremendous relief. It would soon be over—all the fear, guilt, loneliness, aching, longing, heaviness of heart, disappointment, and despair would be past. The future held promise of peace, security, and love for eternity with Christ. Soon I would be with him!

That is when I died.

Physically, I survived the suicide attempt. Three days in critical condition on the Intensive Care Unit, followed by five more on the medical ward, had done the trick. My body was breathing, talking, eating, walking, smiling, and even laughing. By the end of that period, my entire being was worn out from chatting with the women whose job it was to keep an eye on me around-the-clock.

Nevertheless, I was dead.

One afternoon, a hospital psychiatrist brought with her a journal and a pen. "Write," she said.

"Why not?" I figured. "It is something to do."

Recording this journey began that day.

On the Slab

1-21

My first full day out of Intensive Care. All my reserves of physical energy and mental vigor are sapped. Nevertheless, perfunctory conversation includes humor and empty laughter. Meaningless voices chat amiably and some express their own sorrow. By listening kindly, I add to my own hurt.

One after another, shift followed by shift for the last three days, nurses and suicide guards rotate into and out of the room. Each asks myriad questions and offers nonprofessional advice. Headaches instantaneously arise with the possibility of yet another conversation. The tiniest of decisions, and even vague thoughts about life continuing tomorrow, cause pounding in my skull.

I feel responsible, guilty, for not being friendly enough. I want people to stop asking anything of me.

Such a busy hospital ward. Why is it no one in this spinning crowd hears me desperately screaming? I once believed it was selective hearing on the part of others, yet maybe it is that I am not screaming aloud.

1-24

Finally, it is off to the Psych ward.

Pleasantly, street clothes are the uniform on this floor and I am doubly relieved to discover I have a private room and am off suicide watch. To my surprise, it is a little challenging to face even this secluded society without a buffer. I tense at the loudness of an apparently enthused soon-to-be-released fifteen-year-old girl. Unfortunately, there is only a community dining space and eating privately in my room is not an option. Personal hygiene, laundry, and making my bed are my duties; these responsibilities seem overwhelming.

The only group meeting remaining on today's schedule is a wrap-up about whether or not anyone reached their daily goal. Since I am new, I do not have to answer; and I determine to have a planned response tomorrow to avoid actually interacting with anyone.

My thoughts wander to going home to the apartment I share with my husband. Facing repeated cycles is inevitable. I do not want to get well and go around again. I want to die and, in actuality, "go home."

1-25

Decisions between life or death have been made before. Twice. Each one tilted in favor of survival at the last minute. Ambivalence is what kept me from pulling the trigger in a farmer's field twenty-four years ago. Spiritual questioning followed by the cry, "God if you want me to live you will have to stop this" is why the razor was set aside years later during round two. This time however, ambivalence and doubt were absent, replaced with certainty and determination. A peaceful pall lingered for three days after making this choice and following through with the suicide attempt.

Death was hopefully imminent. I waited, trying to keep appearances as normal as possible. Frustrated my effort did not appear to be working; I allowed the secret of my intentions to escape. Then, immediately regretting that confession, one final, rushed and driven act landed me here. People began asking me why.

For nine days, this desire to die has not changed. I am simply wide-eyed surprised to be facing more decisions I thought I had put behind me for good. "What will you do to feel better?" "How can you keep this from happening again?"

Of course, I do not care. Inside I have already ceased living. I have no idea how to come back from the dead.

1-26

Spider plants are survivors. They are perfect for households where watering follows a pattern of long dry spells interrupted by rare torrential soakings. My old spider plant suffered a year of absolute neglect before finally turning brown. Yet even then, sparse shades of green lingered, offering remote possibilities of a revival. It would have required much tedious nurturing on my part to bring that plant back to life, if it were possible at all. Maybe that is step one to my own resurrection—to find a caretaker with a lot of time on his or her hands. It is tough to do when I would rather be dead. I do not really see the point.

1-27

Choosing life over death is a no-brainer for most people. Life for them seems the better alternative to darkness, nothingness, the unknown, or even hell. However, for some of us the comparison is not so simple. Life equals pain and death seems a relief. The question is whether the pain of living exceeds one's tolerance capabilities. The idea of death may grow in a person's mind from 'inevitable' to 'tomorrow's option' to 'today's necessity'.

Reflecting back, I recognize that since my teens, death has been more of a "tomorrow's option" kind of concept. "Suicide is wrong!" I can shout into the air. An advocate for the sanctity of human life, I have expressed dismay over abortion, capital punishment, genocide, and euthanasia. Nevertheless, fragments of a death wish float closely behind those words.

A combination of onslaughts against my own sense of purpose in recent times includes my husband Jerry's and my move to Philadelphia from Cleveland one year ago. Jerry obtained a good job here and we arrived on New Year's Day. Those last months in Ohio were ones of closure as I left two part-time positions that I loved, and said goodbye to numerous friends and to the women and children I mentored. In November, I completed my full-time schooling, and December spun as we feverishly packed and prepared to sell the house.

After helping to unpack the moving truck's contents into our apartment, our grown sons who did not wish to leave their friends or town said their goodbyes to us at the door. They were heading back to Cleveland, and it would be months before we would see them again. I woke up the next day with nothing to do. My life had gone from sixty mph to zero mph literally overnight. I was exhausted, burned-out, and lonely. Soon our marriage struggles resumed, and combined with the emptiness of my days, my mood started to turn downward fast.

•• • ● •••

Earlier this month, having sought professional mental health care only a few weeks ago, my new therapist, Kelly, recommended I attend Dr. Jason (Jay) Baruti's four days per week, two hours per day Intensive Outpatient Program (IOP). I had still been trying a little to survive. I remember liking the people and interacting where I could.

The second day of IOP is when I confessed to the group that many years ago while reaching for a drinking glass, an oh-so-familiar spiteful voice had bellowed in my head, "You don't deserve glass. Look how pretty it is. You're not good enough for it. Use cheap-like-you plastic." Obeying in simple agreement, I had chosen the plastic cup.

Dr. Jay commented, "If someone else were to say they do not deserve to drink from a glass cup, I think you would disagree with them."

"Of course. I would tell them to go to the store and buy the fanciest glass cup they could find and use it every day," I replied.

"And you could do that for yourself," he added hopefully.

Three days after his suggestion, on Friday afternoon, is when I went to the local thrift store and tried to enter the aisle of kitchenware. It was as if some all-consuming sense of horror inside me was screaming, "You can't go down that aisle! That's not for the likes of you!"

Intensely self-loathing, a peaceful future seemed out of reach. At best, I knew living would temporarily feel better and then return to this place of desperate loneliness and pain. At worst, there would be no reprieve at all. "Tomorrow's option" had become "today's necessity," and either way, there seemed no reason not to choose death, so I chose it.

••●••

It is already nearing two weeks from the day I gave up, and I am just now beginning to lose my shock at being alive. As I see it, the future is dark. Nothing is worth the fight anymore, and since my suicide attempt failed to reach its ultimate end, I do not know what to do.

My outward appearance changes throughout the day; I am an unclean hermit and then suddenly I am an organizer straightening up my room, doing laundry, taking a shower. Rarely am I somewhat social. Engaging in bit conversations while offering weak smiles and absent-minded laughter, intermittently I remember I am supposed to be deceased, which always puts a damper on any enthusiasm.

I wonder just how the walking dead are supposed to act, anyway.

SITTING UP

1-27

Options. Where there have seemed to be none, now
there are two.

I have been thinking today about how to get away
with suicide here; how maybe I could join forces with
the "Energizer Bunny," a woman who untiringly and
fiercely walks up and down the halls, mumbling and
sometimes yelling she is going to find a way to kill
herself. On the other hand, I could choose Kelly's idea
and tell my caretakers what I am plotting.

Several patients are trying so hard to be positive
they must have forgotten they are on the psych ward.
They play cards, crack jokes, buy pizza for everyone, and
generally make a lot of noise. Why are they still here?
It is irritating to watch people be happy. Some partiers

are going home tomorrow, and I hope it will be quieter for a while.

Emotional exhaustion comes easily. I freeze if anyone asks me a personal question or asks me how my day is going. Laughter leads to such a pit of emptiness; it feels as if I have fallen into a cavern.

Maybe it is just a need for air. A Navy Seal might hold his breath underwater for long minutes at a time following a major catastrophe on land. Eventually, the pressure becomes too great and he has to risk everything for a gulp of air. However, for me, resurfacing from suffocating despair for that brief second only serves to remind me of the surrounding threatening state, and I sink below once more, not sure I ever care to breathe again.

I guess the theory around here is to keep swimming and gasping and eventually the desire to return to land will resume. I get that. It is just that I am beyond caring to reach that day. I want my struggle to be over—to finally exhale and sink slowly to the bottom to rest among the rocks.

Tomorrow I will not talk to anybody.

1-29

In the early dawn, I dreamed of a man's angry face hovering over mine. Disgusted and unconcerned, in a firm voice he said, "You know you can have no further contact with me. Ever."

My anguish was intense and I awoke already weeping. Thoughts whirled in despair around what I painfully believe follows openness in any relationship, the dismissal. People always leave. Lying on my bed facing the wall, unresponsive to my psychiatrist except to mumble, "I'm going to do it," has caused twenty-four hour watch to resume. The naive guard, new to the job, was easy to deceive, and by noon I had tried once again to end my life.

This evening I heard the changing of my guard take place. Three women quietly gossiped about the psych ward nurses as I lay curled up under my covers listening. The protector whose job it is to stand vigil over me complained that no one would allow her to sleep.

Pent-up anger slowly rose in me, triggered by her carelessness. Weak protests created just enough energy to stand, then to grumble at a nurse as she dealt out meds, wash my laundry, and eat a delayed dinner.

Go figure. Maybe the walking dead are supposed to get mad.

1-30

Jerry visited today. He gave me a letter apologizing for his failings in loving me as God commands, promising to encourage my friendships and to spend time with me regularly. He said he wants me to work at writing, not because of potential income, but because it is what I believe God has asked of me.

I could not remember a time he has encouraged me to do something I want to do. He responded that is because he is a bum and then cried. It is an uplifting thought that creativity could become a staple in my life. We talked about the upcoming in-hospital family meeting and the possibility of incorporating outside help for our relationship. These conversations held a lot of promise; nevertheless, we have had marital resurrections before. It never takes long to fail to love well. If I am to have any hope, the future *must* include permanent accountability with a marriage counselor.

1-31

"Turquoise Klepto" keeps wandering in and out of people's rooms and stealing clothes. "Screaming Man" is adamantly doing what my nickname for him implies, while "Creepy Carl," my most recent suicide watch guard, tells me he is "usually peaceful" after describing his explosive experiences with anger. These people, along with anticipating the family meeting, have me shaking and feeling nauseous. I want to hide but fear there is no longer any safe place to go.

•• • ● • ••

Surrounded by four men during the family meeting, it is intimidating being a focus of discussion. My mind's eye envisions their ferocious faces hovering mere inches above mine scolding, and threatening. In reality, their expressions are kind as they sit across the room. This horror is because I am fearful of exposure, of letting other people know who I actually am. There is always a price to pay for revealing one's heart, and this foreboding is nearly paralyzing.

I have to disappear! I have to curl up and hide! There is no safe place but sleep. At least in the unconscious world I will not know I am afraid. If attacked, perhaps I can sleep through it and remain unaware. I must hide! After all, the walking dead do not belong to the daylight.

FEET ON THE FLOOR

1-31

Was Lazarus of the New Testament distressed that Jesus summoned him back to life? I would be. Moreover, I would want to understand why a loving God would expect me to like his choice. I know this is how I would feel because he is actually calling me back from the dead and it is terrifying. It is as if I am sitting on the edge of a stone slab in my tomb, linen-wrapped feet dangling just above the floor, afraid to stand up. I can choose to lie back down, ignore his voice, and refuse to emerge. Or I can put my feet on the floor.

I wonder how long Lazarus pondered before he made his choice. Perhaps he heard Jesus call, thought he was on his way to paradise, and after enthusiastically passing through the tomb exit, was surprised to find himself still on this difficult planet, his tortured sisters greeting him. What a bombshell! It is easy to imagine he might have attended therapy for years after that day, trying to readjust to the living world!

More likely, he was aware what had been asked of him. It takes faith to put dead feet on the floor. It requires courage I am not sure I have.

But Jesus is calling.

His voice is in my psychiatrist's efforts at keeping me alive. It is in the tears of my husband who says he wants me home and safe. It is in the lack of means of successfully harming myself on the psych ward, and in the new flicker of possibility called marriage counseling. Today I remain uncertain. Death still seems the wiser choice over re-emerging into the turmoil of life.

Lazarus had reason to be frustrated when he was called out of his grave. In my opinion, he had reason to question why his friend and Savior drew him out of peaceful rest and back into indefinite struggle. Jesus, having once been asked to leave heaven in order to walk this pain-filled earth, would have understood those feelings.

Perhaps that is why he wept.

2-1

I almost escaped! My guard fell asleep and I made it all the way to the squeaky door of my room without her waking. Yet alas, she jumped up as I pushed it open. Oh, the temptation to run from her! How I long for just a few private moments. These watchers make me nervous with their inquiries at the change of every shift. They want to know what I did to end up here, how I became suicidal, what family I have, and why I am so sad. No, these people are not therapists; they are men and women with the part-time job of sitting with patients like me. Their duty is to remain within three feet of me at all times. At *all* times.

They get bored and want to unload. I am exasperated most hours of the day by their stories and frustrations, tireless questions, and rehashing of recent history. Unbelievably, my only escape is talking with the actual professionals. I try to ignore the guards, and to slip into sleep as much as possible. Their varying degrees of understanding and excessive conflicting advice is tedious and makes me upset. I am tempted to lie to my psychiatrist about my condition in order to get rid of them, yet lying is something I firmly refuse to do. As long as my thoughts toy with self-harm, the sentinel will remain.

I have begun to feel them touching me. In bed with my back to them, I can hear them rummaging through my things and talking about me. I turn and there they sit, reading a waiting-room magazine. As paranoia has been creeping in, I tearfully told a nurse I am going insane. Last night I had to ask for a medical doctor because my body was twitching, hurting, nauseous, and shaking.

This morning I begged my psychiatrist to take me off suicide watch. I told him it was as if being tortured, and broken down, I was ready to say, do, sign, or promise anything to get those people away from me. Anything.

Assuring me I need not make any promises, he agreed. Now my motive is to remain free.

•• ● ••

"Who took my money?" It is very late at night, and twenty-two year-old Alex is standing in the middle of the hallway, shouting. "I had money and now it is gone!"

Moments earlier, he had emptied his pockets of change and tossed it to the floor. Another patient picks it up and hands it back to him.

"Thank you," Alex says pleasantly. Within a minute coins are flying once again and he is demanding, "Who took my money?"

Pointing to an approaching nurse, Alex continues rambling. "Take your Lithium, Alex," the nurse is commanding, producing a pill from his hand.

"No. You are not right."

Terrence, a middle-aged man, is greatly troubled at Alex's actions. "People outside these walls won't understand if he acts that way. Alex will embarrass himself and that makes me sad," he said, recalling his own experiences with their shared mental disorder in his youth.

In watching Alex's face, I think he seems sincerely upset even though he is making little sense. I know, as does everyone else in the room, that Alex needs the medication. We have all seen him reasonable, intelligent, articulate, and sane. He is a great kid. Attempting to calm him down and failing reminds me our situations are similar in that tricky diseases have landed us here. These disorders convince us we have no need for medical care. Years ago, an acquaintance of Jerry's and mine stopped his mental health medication intake and lost his life to suicide. This confusion about self-care has also happened to me.

Last spring no one could have convinced me I had misunderstood. Certain God was telling me the antidepressant and mood stabilizers that had kept me generally stable for six years were no longer necessary, I stopped taking them. Almost immediately negative thoughts pummeled any determination to make this work. One month passed, then two. By the time three months was approaching, I was growing increasingly disturbed.

"Will you be able to make it to your car?" A concerned cashier watched as I had difficulty completing a simple transaction.

Barely able to focus my thoughts, I knew as soon as I arrived home what I had to do.

"God," I cried. "I can't do this anymore. I'm going back on meds."

Resuming a half-dose of the original prescription, my mood picked up a little within a few days. "You've disappointed God," my brain lied. "He told you to go off meds and you do not trust him. You never needed that medication. The doctors were wrong." Guilt joined hands with depression to accuse and deceive me.

Another young man, barely twenty-five-years-old, is leaving tomorrow. Justin smiles a lot more than when he first joined this peculiar club. Every day his parents and two brothers came to visit and encourage their beloved. Earlier today, he and I had laughed about the movie, *One Flew Over the Cuckoo's Nest* and instantly agreed on who Nurse Ratchet is in our hospital. The cards he's been dealt mental health-wise are easier to bear than Alex's are, however they can be just as deadly if allowed to carry out their malevolent scheme.

Today my choices are coming into focus: to live, to die, or to live well. Until now, I have been comparing only the first two because I did not believe living well to be a possibility. To live means continuing to do what I have always done before—waiting for Jerry to respond more to my liking, hoping the other shoe fails to drop, and clinging to the presumption of control over my future. To die apparently will hurt people I leave behind, some who love and even need me deeply. On the other hand, maybe another attempt on my life would fail, leaving me maimed or brain-damaged.

To live well means choosing once again to trust, allowing life's challenges to motivate healthy behaviors such as asking for help instead of expecting people innately to know what to do. It also means giving up any idea of suicide. Now I am behaving, just being good. Sometimes I hope for hope. Although concerned I am making a mistake, the energy to end my life has dissipated, replaced with exhaustion. I just want to stay in bed for a few weeks.

2-2

I was surprised to find myself walking along a pretty and peaceful street. Green, leafy oaks lined the sidewalks. Hearing the thunderous plunk of a large ball and the crash of toppled pins, I asked a nearby young girl what was going on. Giggling in her excitement, she said she enjoyed bowling so much her father had built an alley in their backyard. Continuing to pass comfortable homes with manicured lawns, I knew they housed happy families like that of the young girl's.

Looming out over the neighborhood, a towering, white mansion faced the end of the street. It was beautiful in its architecture with stretches of delicate white stone carving and a welcoming archway shading the front door. Thick trees satisfied the empty space against the sky, and I marveled at the building's disproportionate size in comparison to the residences surrounding it. Just behind it lay the mystical "Los Angeles," an enormous city it was everyone's desire to reach. For in the City of Angels, no one was ever sad, and goodness reigned. One had to pass through the expansive house and exit through the back door in order to enter that city of perfect peace.

A very rich elderly man lived in the house. He warmly welcomed me at the front door as I approached, excited to see me. Once inside, the conversation turned to my desire to pass through the back door. He said, "You can't stay. Not yet. It is not time."

I turned, rejoicing in my own future. My new husband was one of a dozen siblings in a large loving family where I was also welcome to be myself. I was cherished by them and considered a part of the whole. Happy and relaxed, I arrived at my new home with its charming yard and content people sprawling over the porch and playing in the grass. I attempted to send a cell phone picture and text to my friends with the words, "My new man and home."

When I tried to capture my happiness in a photograph, the house shrunk to the size and appearance of a shack. The lawn converted into an unkempt, muddy bed littered with old rusty pieces of metal and broken bottles. The now unruly children, my husband's siblings, were dressed in rags. The picture appeared black and white, quickly fading to a dull brown.

I woke up grieving the loss of serenity and joy I had known in this dream. Feeling as if I were on the perimeter of real life, not belonging and barely noticed, I went through the acts of getting dressed and eating breakfast.

Profoundly sad, I saw the disappointing truth—life is full of pain. There is no large, nurturing family loving me and waiting for me to come home. Fathers in the neighborhoods of the real world are not building bowling alleys in their backyards to bring joy to their little girls. There is no perfect spouse, and this earth does not contain the peace I long to know. The photograph is old. My hopes and dreams are faded and I know it is time to put them away. I cannot force them to become reality.

Someday I know I will pass through welcoming gates on my way to a delightful, eternal city and find myself warmly cherished. However, not yet. The hope I had placed in premature death was misplaced. Regardless of what is coming, some of which scares me enormously, I am to rejoin society and work in therapy and marriage counseling in an obedient attempt at doing my best until the Great Day God takes me home.

This morning, like Lazarus, I make the decision to put my feet on the floor. Jesus is calling. "Come forth. Live the life I've given you, and I will be with you always- even to the end of the world."

As dreaded, I believe some good days and many bad, a few achievements and plenty of failures, a little love, and much hurt are in my future. I recognize maybe a small number of days I will feel blessed, content in my marriage, and hopeful for the future.

Nevertheless, I weep.

First Step

2-3

This hurts! I have to stay in my room because Klepto is in my art therapy group, and if I get close to her I'll probably kill her! I am shaking because earlier she was staring at my shoes with covetous eyes. In an attempt at self-protection, I had glared into those eyes and warned, "Don't you even think about it." Now she is going to come in here sometime to filch my possessions. I have to calm down.

A black-haired petite psychiatrist has been sent to check up on me, and is staring at my chart with a painted grin on her stiff face. Her mouth remains in perfect position as if no thoughts have crossed her mind. "You need to cooperate and not play these games," she is chiding without having asked me for an explanation.

"You need to go to art therapy." Her fake half-smile has not changed.

"I am not playing games," I correct her.

The grin continues to speak. "You are not helping yourself by being stubborn."

Her condescension irritates me. Speaking steadily, I inform her, "My nerves are already frazzled and you need to wipe that ridiculous smile off your face. I am not playing games, but you are asking me to. You want me to go out there as if everything is fine. It's not fine. I'm staying in my room to avoid the kleptomaniac because if I see her I may hit her."

A doctoral resident standing nearby praises me for knowing my limits.

The "Energizer Bunny" and I stayed up late last night drawing in one of the children's *Hello Kitty* coloring books. It was all that was available to do at that hour, and we were giggling uncontrollably as we dressed Kitty in a thong and gave her a tattoo and body piercings.

Unfortunately, we could not use art therapy supplies to do Kitty justice. The room where those items are stored is locked and certainly the key is nowhere a patient could find it. After all, there are dangerous items in the art room: paint; children's rounded scissors; clay.

After running out of time at one art session, I asked if I could finish my project in my room. Serious discussion among staff members followed before arriving at the consensus I could have the paper project and a glue stick. No scissors. Since all my pieces had already been cut, that compromise worked for me. The newly dubbed "Nurse Ratchet" walked by.

"You can't have that glue stick!" She was emphatic. "You might eat it."

It would do no good to laugh; she would not understand. The glue stick was non-toxic, no more poisonous than hospital Jell-O, and much less dangerous than the nearby five-foot cord I had been eyeing.

I told my psychiatrist and anyone on his staff who would listen today that I need to leave. It is agreed. Tomorrow I go home. To my earth-home, to our apartment where in and out, in and out breathing will begin, once again concentrating on one moment at a time. I do not see the tomb exit getting any closer or the faint glow from outside growing brighter. Nevertheless, I feel deep relief at leaving the hospital.

If I am hoping beyond that moment, it is the hope this uncomfortable anxiety will go away. I do not look forward to the partial hospitalization and intensive outpatient programs that are to be my next step. You see, when one awakens from the dead, feet still bound in linen strips, motion is slow and tedious. One is likely to be anxious about falling flat on her face.

One important fact remains. Jesus is the one who asked me to rise from the dead. He is standing in the light of day and waiting to receive me back into the land of the living. Once I am there, perhaps his voice will speak clearly to me again and his promise will become my stay. "I will never leave you nor forsake you."[1]

2-4

Partners join forces in three-legged races by tying two legs together, the right of one player and the left of the other. Then they walk as fast as they can to the finish line, stumbling and holding each other up the entire way. However when one falls, so does the other. Few teams make it all the way to the end.

That sounds like marriage.

Jerry was diagnosed with a depressive disorder about the time our second son was born. His symptoms of social withdrawal and irritability had exacerbated our already misguided styles of relating to each other. Somehow, we were still together, driven for right or wrong by a mutual belief that honoring God was to make this union last.

Our marriage has been rough in many respects. Initially we were not kind to each other. Although improvements have come, gone, and come back again, I am afraid. Taking life's journey alone is a scary thought. My distrust and negative outlook played a part in capsizing the progress Jerry and I had made over the last few years, so now what? Trust is not something one pulls out of a bag, tries on for size, and hangs in the closet for later use. Not when the alliance of two desperate and uncertain people is at stake. It has to clothe the union every day, and be the chosen team uniform.

Figuratively, we tie our two legs together, look at each other, and hesitantly grin. We know what is ahead of us, limping, tugging, and expecting the other to keep pace. It is rather likely we will fall, and with each plunge is the danger of injury, loss, and blame. The finish line looks far away but we do not actually know how long it will take us to get there. It is the racing that counts, anyway.

Our eyes meet with an understanding forged over twenty- nine years together. The first wobbly step is taken as we leave the hospital without looking back.

2-5

I was wondering tonight why my stomach is still upset even though I have been home for twenty-four hours. Because of this, I went to bed an hour ago and now am wide-awake. Snoozing in those few minutes gave me several dreams, all of which had someone chasing, harassing, or watching me. When I woke up the paranoia continued. I saw someone at the foot of the bed, heard people in the kitchen, and now I hear footsteps, even though our apartment is empty and carpeted.

I understand why I was being watched so carefully in the hospital considering I pulled out my IV on the second day and tried to kill myself again a little over a week ago. But this is the truth—after a combined total of only fifteen days under relentless scrutiny, I told the doctor I would say, do, or sign anything he wanted me to if he would only make the guards go away. I would make a terrible POW.

As for the tummy pain, it must be anxiety still. I just do not give enough respect to trauma.

2-7

Art therapy had been a return to contented memories filled with the scents of markers, glue, and paint. Creativity is an old friend, faithfully present in former years to shelter me from strong emotions too powerful to bear. It is fitting then that this opportunity for playfulness be reintroduced now. In the hospital, we drew, pasted, and shaped in clay our feelings. I do not actually care about the expression part of it, relishing instead any escape from emotions. I just love designing uses for art supplies.

Anxiety hurts. Physically and emotionally, one is nearly paralyzed by the collection of its indescribable sensations. Oh, there is the typical knot in the stomach, the tension headache, quickened breathing, and shaking. However, the rising panic from unknown origins is most difficult to describe. Today all it took was one thought about the hospital to set off debilitating anxiety.

We shopped at an art supplies store to pick up some colored pencils and clay. Keeping them close-by provides my hands with something productive to do. I am decidedly not busy. The anxiety is alleviated a little as I concentrate on small projects.

Jerry suggested we drive to see the building where I will be attending the partial hospitalization program, also referred to as a day treatment center. It does not look so intimidating. Having never experienced a full-day outpatient therapy setting before, waiting for tomorrow is nerve-racking.

2-14

Five days per week for five and a half hours per day, twenty ne'er-do-wells gather in a crowded room to discuss what brought us here and to practice measuring our suicidal ideation against a numbered chart on the wall.

"I'm a four," one young man says. He looks to be about twenty-years-old, and a few of the older women baby him.

Four is high on the chart. Four means he has the desire and the means to kill himself. However, one point shy of five, he expresses no plan or intent. Today I am a three, a middle ground that describes having a powerful death wish and no means or intent to carry it through. Both of us are asked what we will do to stay safe until our return the next morning.

"I'll stay near and talk with my family," he promises. I add, "I'll draw."

2-18

The therapist assigned to my case at the partial hospitalization program, the woman who has barely spoken to me in the eight days of my attendance, is smiling sweetly and showing off the individualized treatment plan she designed.

"I just need you to sign here, and here," she said as she pointed.

This paper read of improvements in mood that lacked substantial evidence. Maybe I was smiling too much. On my inside, heavy pressure and near-terror controlled each word I spoke. Familiar sadness slowed every movement.

At some level, I resented this person making judgment calls based on information I did not think she had. Earlier she had behaved unprofessionally when she entered the support group room half-filled with addicts on their way to rehab, expressing her frustration.

"I need a drink or something!" She sighed as she grabbed a chair. "I think the reason I'm so stressed is because I've never been high."

Still, I sign the discharge papers. On my way out the door, I drop off a written complaint. It is disappointing and dangerous when the professionals are not good at their jobs.

Looking Back at the Slab

2-22

There is a powerful difference between walking out of duty versus out of desire. I am in no hurry. Powerful negative emotions seem to control my mind still, and such emptiness and hopelessness swell in my spirit. Knowing all will not be well in the light, I teeter forward, trusting the snail pace of re-entry will protect me from losing my balance.

A familiar brash, threatening voice fills my ears. It has been with me as long as I can remember, and maliciously turns my thoughts to self-loathing. *It must be hard work for people to care what is underneath, to see me. I guess I have to be eternally indebted to anyone who smiles at me, is kind to me, or wants to be my friend. It is charity work after all. Only the professionals are paid.*

Figuratively, I am in a car wash without a car. Brush strokes are scratching me raw, boiling soap saturates the wounds. Buffeted by powerful forces, I do not know peace or sleep. Emotionally battered, burned, and nearly drowned, the past few months have been torture. Jerry told me he loves me, and I asked him why. The only answers he could give were typical: he appreciates my friendship and caretaking. I want to hear about qualities that are unique to me.

If I were to make the list for myself, I would write at least a dozen traits like funny, straightforward, compassionate, and creative. It is doubtful I will ever see such a list from my husband, and so the emotions roll. If the harsh voice in my head will not be quiet, I need Jerry's assurances of love to be louder.

At present, tomorrow's meeting with Dr. Jay, whose phone call last month resulted in my admission to the hospital despite my protests, is especially disconcerting.

The ringing of the phone had interrupted my internet searching for a more efficient means of suicide.

"Hello, Nancy," Dr. Jay had begun. "Did you hurt yourself?"

"Yes," I admitted reluctantly.

"What did you do?"

"I don't want to say." Of course, eventually I answered this question and he offered an ultimatum.

"I will have to call 911 unless you agree to take yourself to the hospital."

"I don't want to go. What do you care, anyway? This won't change your life any!"

Steadily, he replied, "I don't think you can say that with any certainty."

"Why do you care? You don't know me."

"When I meet someone I tend to care about them."

This resonated as a familiar experience. People I meet tend to become instantly important to me at some level as well. My reply came hesitantly. "I can understand that. I do that too."

Long silence followed as I realized my chance of escape was slipping away. Options rushed through my brain. Running away from the police would inevitably end quickly. There was nowhere to hide. Was there a means to end my life before the police showed up? Ideas were eliminated one after the other as too slow, containing too few guarantees.

"Please don't do this," I begged. "I don't want to go to the hospital."

"I have to call 911 unless you agree to take yourself." My only two choices.

"What if I won't go?"

"Then the police will make a scene at your home for all your neighbors to see."

Sighing through another long pause, I felt cornered. An uncomfortable scene in our new apartment complex was not a pleasant thought—if I was going to live to see the results that is. Unable to find a way out, it seemed a good idea at least to inquire about the hospitals in the area. After serving my time, I could do as I pleased.

Following our agreement that I would go to the nearby Emergency Room he recommended, Dr. Jay invited me back to IOP. "I'll be glad to see you when you come back."

"I don't know," I said with another sigh.

•• ● ••

Calling Jerry to tell him he had to take me to the hospital raised worry in his voice. "What is going on?" he asked.

My answer was cryptic. "Nothing. Dr. Jay just said I have to go."

Jerry had to deal with this limited information until we found ourselves waiting at the ER. His response was concerned and firm as he sat with me through doctor reports and prognoses.

I am not proud of my words to either of them that day, and seeing Dr. Jay again will be mortifying. It is a scary proposition to face the man who essentially saved my life, considering before his interruption I intended to do more to end it. I am not grateful, yet anyway, and may never be completely.

Tomorrow I return to IOP. It is tempting to go back to the slab.

2-24

"Hello," Dr. Jay greets me with a smile.

"What happened to you?" I have glanced up to see he is on crutches, and this affords me an easy icebreaker. Under normal circumstances, I would not be relieved someone is hurt; nevertheless, on this anxiety-pummeled day I am glad we have something to talk about besides me. Any other icebreaker would have done nicely, so I guess I am not totally heartless!

Paperwork nearly fills the next fifteen minutes, but not before Dr. Jay asks how I am doing. We discuss how I was once dead, have since sat up and placed my feet on the floor, and we agree the goal is that I always look forward. My sincerity is questionable.

How did I end up in this place again? I do not want to be here or anywhere, and cannot believe I am expected to continue to fight for the life I gave up on a short few weeks ago. On the surface, it appears other group members and I have gathered for one reason—to get our emotions under control and move on with successful, happy living. Nevertheless, I am not here to get well.

I am here to be good; to obey hospital psychiatrists, the psychologist in front of me, and ultimately God, who I doubt is happy with me just now. Getting well means jumping back onto the relationships spiral, riding out another round of trust only to have it hurt again. There is no reason to believe this perception of loved then unloved will ever end. I do not want to be in the cycle anymore.

Growing up in the country, my job was to keep the creek clean and flowing after thunderstorms. Fallen branches, stirred mud, and dead leaves would wind their way downstream only to become clogged inside a tunnel of unyielding cement walls. It was there, under the roadway bridge, where I spent many an hour in boots, raking and tugging away at the debris in hopes of freeing the water from its piled dam. Now, similarly to the motionless creek, a raging storm of disappointment and fear has left me at a standstill. I am in need of the desire to face another day. IOP is offering the tools for finding hope, joy, and purpose.

I am resisting, certain none of those things are for me. Not this time around.

2-25

"Just because we aren't doing something to hurt ourselves doesn't mean we aren't depressed," someone is saying. It is a cold Friday morning.

"Smiles and laughter do not equal 'all better,'" Dr. Jay agrees. " People see the function and don't understand the depression."

"It's annoying when people dismiss my emotions," a young man says. "'Oh', they say when I am upset at them, 'You need to take your meds!' Then I tell them, 'If I take my meds you will still be a jerk!'"

Laughter fills the room defying logic in light of the powerfully wavering emotions we feel. A woman observes about me, "You strike me as quick to smile, and fun. I'm surprised to hear you say you'd rather be dead."

That is why people do not get it.

Sometimes even I do not get it and can combat trying to feel better out of fear I am just kidding myself. I believe good emotions are fake because they will certainly not last.

"What if they are real?" Dr. Jay asks. "What if they are not fake?"

Cognitive Behavioral Therapy (CBT) is new to me. CBT is based on the premise that thoughts and behaviors influence feelings. Therefore, learning to recognize and focus on what is encouraging, and acting in ways that will promote who we want to be, will eventually bring about emotions that are more positive.

Rather than shuffling through mental leaves of history concentrating on what created our distress, CBT focuses on the solution, the improvement of our present mood. One such tool is asking the question, "What if?"

According to Dr. Jay, applying "what if" to our reactions to our feelings can bring about behavior that actually helps us feel better. "What if I can respond in a way that honors my values? What if acting opposite of how I feel lessens my suffering?"

"If we look at the negative aspects of our situation such as 'no one is there for me', we will feel depressed," he continues. "Then we may perpetuate our loneliness by isolating in response. Since we can have a positive effect on our thoughts and behaviors, which in turn will influence our emotions, what is one opposite action you could take?"

His questions call us to refuse being helpless victims of mental diseases. I am not ready to jump into this battle! Which will I choose today? Actions that will help lift my mood?

On the other hand, maybe I will go back to bed.

Another Small Step Forward and Half Step Back

3-1

Recovery from Major Depression and a suicide attempt is like following a continuum. At the farthest point is the end goal: fully functioning in society; experiencing and developing healthy relationships; finding purpose in life; wanting to live; joy. In traveling up the continuum, sometimes one will go forward, and sometimes back. The process to the end goal will take time; for many of us the trip is indefinite. Today, my goal is to go up one notch on that continuum, and to avoid what will send me backward. Anything more than that is overwhelming. Perhaps one reason why my journey so

NANCY VIRDEN

far has been ambivalent is my expectations are to move on too far, too fast.

Suddenly two days ago at the prompting of fellow IOP members, I did it! Entering a kitchenware aisle and forcing myself to make a choice, I selected a unique drinking glass and brought it home. It is pretty. I held it up to the light to show to Jerry, and then set it in the kitchen window. It is still not for me. Somehow, it must have been smuggled into my house against all rules of proper conduct.

Where did I learn such self-hatred? At what point in my life did I cease to believe I deserve to live well and to love who I am?

Metaphorically focusing on the tomb's exit, my eyes squint against the blinding light that is outside, contrasting with the surrounding darkness with which I have grown comfortable. In the real world, sparkles stream across the windowsill through the forbidden glass. I do not have to drink out of it today. I tried something new in buying it, which was good enough. In fact, I think I will use it to hold my colored pencils, drawing being such a regular source of positive distraction.

3-8

Like ocean waves, powerful thoughts rise and fall, gain in strength and wane. Clouds of emotions gather and dispel. In one week, they have traveled from anxiety and discouragement to relaxation and hope, and back again. What set off negativity this time? A slew of

56

disappointments in the form of what I perceive to be rejection.

"Is it important to get over past hurts?" someone asks.

"Yes" Dr. Jay answers. "Do you want to?"

"I'd like to let it go."

"Then why don't you?" he prods.

"I don't want to let my abuser get away with it. No one is holding him accountable and what he has done is not right!" she adds.

Dr. Jay pursues his point. "When you are holding onto something, it affects you. Letting go gives you the freedom to think positive thoughts about yourself and the situation."

"It's not the same as letting him off the hook," another group member says. "But it allows you to move on."

"Some people are never going to change," I break in absent-mindedly as I doodle. "It doesn't matter what you say or how you say it, they are going to remain as they are. All we can do is draw boundaries and declare, 'You are not going to do this to me, not this time. I decide when it happens again—I choose what day I will visit you or talk to you.' Knowing what the cost is."

"What are you holding onto today, Nancy?" Dr. Jay turns to me.

"It has more to do with my marriage."

"Seems like quite a struggle."

"You were more talkative the other day," a doctoral intern observes.

Silence follows. "I don't want to disclose anything," I finally say.

"Without being specific, can you tell how it is affecting you?" Dr. Jay asks.

"I feel like crap." My pen scribbles nearly uncontrollably because my hand is shaking.

"What's been your reaction to feeling like crap?" he presses.

I shrug and continue to draw. "I'm not going to share that."

After a few more evasive answers on my part, Dr. Jay states, "Nancy, you're in charge of how much you let out."

"Then I guess I'm done."

No one in the room knows the enormity of what I am hiding. One part of it is since Jerry had been in one sort of church ministry or another throughout our marriage, I had had years of practicing the art of staying mum about what took place in our house. Sadly, we who are married to a missionary or church leader often hold ourselves in deeper confines than most people seem to understand. How dare we express concern over our marriage in a church Bible Study?

What would people think of our spouse's leadership if we told anyone about last night's fight? Our depression, our partner's depression, our relationship struggles, personal unforgiving, and so on remain poisonous secrets. All too often, we curl up inside ourselves and outwardly smile. I silenced myself to protect his reputation and to prevent my humiliation. It is uncertain I can learn to do any differently.

IOP closes for the day and everyone walks out. Left behind is a doodle of a pile of manure with my name on it.

3-9

From what I am hearing, it appears those same three choices remain to live, to die, or to live well. Which one do I really want? Suicide remains an inviting concept, yet brings along with it punishing baggage to carry for those left behind. A friend tells me of her father's death by his own hand. She is still angry at the loss, the "what might have been." Moreover, it has been over thirty years.

However, right now I am just living, stuck between desiring and escaping change. So much of me wants to pour out what has been held in for decades. Fear of exposure prevents it in this group setting. I need to see my individual therapist, Kelly, again. Because I have been informed insurance will not cover visits with both individual therapists and IOP, it has been months since speaking with her. Meanwhile, misery is my companion, relationships are at an uncomfortable standoff.

It is terrible being so distant from a spouse in the same room. Jerry is my first love; his attention means nearly everything to me. I suffocate in the separation and then pour more loneliness over my gasping head by maintaining the distance through anger, distrust, or despair.

Ambivalence is the enemy. One day I decide to step forward, the next to pacify my hopelessness by ruminating on sad thoughts. One of the first IOP lessons I took to heart is the concept of recognizing my needs and finding ways to meet them myself. Consequently, I signed up for an art class, launched a freelance writing career, and risked inviting new friends into my world. Yet my feelings remain the same. Looking onward, then back, pivoting in my tracks, it is decision by indecision. Refusing to make up my mind to pursue living well equals an automatic default to old patterns.

I am getting tired of feeling like only so much dung. A choice has to be made.

Sigh. Guess I might as well see about building a less dismal life.

3-17

Taking control of conflicting emotions and following through with processes I am learning in IOP include creating healthy distractions from depressive thoughts such as opening the blinds in my apartment each day, playing positive, upbeat music in the background, writing short to-do lists including art for relaxation along with minor chores, and trying my best to complete each task. Violent television triggers high anxiety and self-destructive urges, so it is avoided.

"While distractions from depressive and anxious thoughts are good, they are temporary. It is the fear you remain focused on, your negative beliefs that feed depression. These need to be let go," Dr. Jay says.

This is not easy to hear. Apparently, perceptions and assumptions that have influenced my emotions all my life are to be changed. Careful introspection reveals surprising, deeply rooted negative beliefs: it is shameful to be weak; shameful to expose strong emotions; I will never be good enough; people are false; I am always guilty of something; and women are only worth what men say they are worth. Where these beliefs originated is uncertain.

"Challenging negative beliefs means deliberately searching for evidence of the positive and not dismissing it," Dr. Jay adds. "We cannot eliminate negative thoughts. They are going to come. However, we can learn to choose which thoughts to hang onto."

"For example, if someone does you harm you may believe 'people cannot be trusted.' However, the evidence tells you there are many people who are trusted by their friends and families. At this point you can choose to focus on the damage done to you which reinforces the belief that people cannot be trusted, or you can focus on the trustworthy people you see around you and begin to challenge that old belief."

This "letting it go" battle appears endless. Nevertheless, I am gambling that robbing negative beliefs of their power will make them diminish over time.

3-21

The last day of IOP. I apologize to Dr. Jay for accusing him of not caring when he called me in January. It is unnerving to consider facing life without the daily support of this group. With few acquaintances in Pennsylvania and those relationships being new, I am shaky at the prospect of going home and it being just Jerry and me again in this strange new place.

Then there are always people who I hope mean well, who continue to chide and correct me when I try to share any struggles. It is encouraging to know Kelly is waiting to pick up where IOP has left off. Dr. Jay's last challenge to me is to pay attention to what he calls "red flags of depression." He suggests if I can observe certain behaviors that signal my mood is sinking, then I can counteract with a positive plan of action and interrupt the downward spiral.

Yeah, we will see.

3-31

Having drawn bright red flags waving high in the sky, I taped the following list to the bottom of the picture.

Warning Signs Depression Is Coming:

1. Isolating: not calling friends back, cancelling plans, avoiding people
2. Negativity: complaining, focusing more on negative beliefs and thoughts like, "This is not worth it"; "It will never get better"
3. Low activity level: less interested in hobbies, staying in bed, frittering time away
4. Ask: How long have these red flags been waving? More than two days? How intensely do I feel

these things? If I sense I am reaching a 7 on a downward scale of 10-1, it is time to interrupt the backslide.

5. Plan of Action: Do not shrug off this mood as unimportant or deny it is happening! Regardless of feelings to the contrary, keep moving; avoid free time; remember all the cons to reaching point 1; connect with people in some way; pray; refocus toward positive thoughts by writing down what I am grateful for; proactively find ways to get my own needs met.

This list is now hanging at the top of closet doors in my office where I will easily see it every day. My new strategy, the "Mental Health Wall" has been established.

4-2

Several small, newsprint covered tables seemed a natural fit surrounded by paint and adhesive bottles, brushes, and piles of decorative papers all crammed into a tiny room. Today held my first collage class at a local art center. A woman other class members would later refer to as "unhealthy," entered the room and approached the teacher.

"I just want to sit off by myself and listen today. I don't want to get involved in any projects," she said in an anxious tone.

The teacher was puzzled. "What we are doing today isn't difficult. I'm sure you will feel comfortable."

"No," the woman insisted. "I've been up all night very upset about the tsunami in Japan; I can't handle any pressure at all."

"There will be no pressure," the teacher said. "You won't find the assignments to be hard."

Taking a deep breath, the increasingly nervous woman measured her words. "You don't understand. I'm asking you to let me sit by myself and just listen today. That is all I can do. If there is going to be pressure to make anything, I will have to leave."

Both women's voices were growing tight and higher pitched. Now the teacher was upset. "I don't understand what you are worried about. I have all your supplies and this is the introductory class. You will be fine with what you undertake."

"I knew I shouldn't have come! This is too much!" The woman spun on her heels and nearly ran out.

Shaken, the teacher's eyes watered and she turned to the rest of us. "That has never happened to me before," she whispered.

"You did all right," one classmate assured her. "It's not your fault."

In my view, a woman had come in courage and presented a simple request. She knew her emotional limits and was asking if she could work within those parameters. Unfortunately, many people do not recognize when this is happening. Instead of being met where she was and allowed to begin art class on her terms, the teacher was insisting she "get with the program." Having paid a high price for trying, the anxious woman had little choice but to leave, no doubt feeling worse.

I wonder if she may have been right; she should not have come.

4-3

An old acquaintance I have not communicated with for over six years has recently contacted me asking how I am doing. Because past conversations centered around our mutual mental health issues, I feel free to talk with her. Besides, I am desperately lonely.

Dear Rose,

Yes, I have a lot of anger. The anger is about not being good enough for significant people in my life. You might think I am a monster and that not all these people could be wrong. Although I know it cannot be true, I suspect it is right. So, most of the anger is at me.

I appreciate what you said about Christ. It makes me cry to know he cares so much for me. However, I also think I am disappointing him by being depressed, not shaking it off fast enough, and not following through on the CBT skills as I should. If my thoughts are under my control, then as one of his children I should be able to get my head up, right? I need to "take every thought captive," think on the good and noble things, consider others' interests as much as my own, and so forth. Since I am failing at all the above and more, I am not certain he is weeping *with* me as you suggest.

Nancy

4-4

Unsuccessful attempts at reaching out to therapists in years past have left me a bit tentative. Not everyone in the helping professions is competent or even in the right job. What I see here is different. The concept of managing my depression rather than just helplessly riding it out is good.

Nonetheless, now that I am out of IOP, I am discovering CBT practiced in a hard-nosed fashion seems a kind of invalidation. My psychiatrist in the hospital did much for me because he just listened. It was only for ten minutes a day, but he carefully picked up on what I said and was able to repeat back to me the gist of it. At one point he said, "I get it. You don't care. You don't care!" I could not believe it. I was actually in shock that someone heard me. "I don't care what happens to me," usually receives responses like "That's the depression talking" or "You will care again someday." To have someone accept what I said at face value was priceless.

Kelly is a hard-nosed CBT therapist and is forever redirecting our conversations. I actually have to plow through, slightly rudely, to get out what I need to say because she is trying so hard to keep me positive. "That's in the past. What is going on today?"

Getting well is a long, intimidating journey stretching before my eyes. Somehow, I have to distance myself for a time from those whose mission it seems is to scold me into immediate "proper" thinking. Some of this is my fault as my perceptions are questionable. Emotional reasoning can lead me to believe if something is felt, it must be true. Still, I may be right in thinking that some people, tired of my slow recovery, are frustrated.

In one phone call, a concerned old friend told me it was a spiritual flaw for me to seek counseling. According to her, my trust is to be in the Lord and him only. Another correspondent told me to get over negative memories. What these well-intended people do not seem to understand is it is impossible for one with bound hands and feet to swim. Waves will carry the dead who are in process of resurrection wildly back and forth until someone comes alongside and conveys them to shore.

This relationship with Kelly is not working out for more than one reason. Desperate to empty an overflowing pot of unspoken history, trust is difficult as it is. Having to fight for it is impossible.

I am on my own again. There may be no one to talk to, perhaps that is my lot. Searching for another counselor is beyond my scope of energy. I guess I can try to do what makes me feel a little bit better and avoid those situations and people who make my suffering worse.

4-6

Because the bank changed my credit card number, an email from Dr. Jay arrived yesterday asking me for the new one. He inquired as to how I have been doing and asked for a reply. It was perfect timing in that earlier in the morning I had left a message on Kelly's voicemail explaining I would not be returning to see her.

> Dr. Jay,
>
> It is a pleasant surprise to hear from you this morning even though you are just begging for money (kidding!). I will call with my credit card info later today.
>
> Art/collage is going great. I am learning all the techniques which is what I wanted to learn, but besides that, I am getting out of the apartment and spending time with people. Writing is keeping me somewhat busy at the moment as I have two deadlines coming up soon.
>
> On the flip side, I am profoundly sad and angry. All the good stuff is tainted with emotional pain. In regular conversation, I am choking back sobs, nothing is as fun as it could be, and my feet are dragging on the most basic of responsibilities. I am still walking; I just need someone to walk with for a while. Kelly is not going to be that person. I called her today and told her I am not coming back. Although I feel we have each given it our best shot, we are not clicking and I am not receiving the help I need.
>
> Nancy

Today, Dr. Jay offered to find a therapist for me if I would like to write down what I am hoping to find. This is new! I had no idea of this option—actually to ask for what one wants in a counselor. I wonder if someone who meets these criteria could be out there somewhere.

4-19

Dear Rose,

The book you sent to me makes me sad because I feel like this author believes that if anyone would just follow steps 1-2-3, they will be well. I need someone to listen to me. I do not want to do steps 1-2-3, I just want to be heard. Actually, I feel like a failure for not having "succeeded" at completing suicide. I wish I had.

Nancy

Dear Nancy,

You said you wish you had succeeded. Tell me more about that...

Rose

Dear Rose,

I quit because I was tired. I was tired of the fight it has always been to be in my head. Tired of feeling unloved, unaccepted, and unapproved. Nothing God could use me for, nothing of all the good I may have to live for seemed worth it anymore. There were too many relational losses, too many more such losses to come.

CBT is all about changing your beliefs by learning new ways of thinking. I am doing what they tell me to do; reading, making charts, thinking constructively, moving despite how I feel, and even having a little fun. But I still *do not care*!

And that is why I wish I had succeeded at dying. Period.

Nancy

4-25

Five days ago, an email from Dr. Jay introduced me to Lynne Cannenta, who has been a therapist for over twenty years. Today I met with her for the first time and was impressed. It was not her professional demeanor that made an impact on me, although she has that. It was not her skill at asking good questions, her patience with my slowness at filling out forms, or her warmth that makes me want to go back. These attributes are there in abundance. However, it is one moment, a few seconds at the end of our session that determine for me this relationship is worth pursuing.

She handed me a paper that looked to have listed as many as dozens of mental health goals and asked me to circle which ones I hoped to meet through therapy.

A quick glance showed me none of it mattered. The answer I wanted to circle was not there.

Briskly passing the paper back to her I said, "I don't care about any of these."

"What do you want?" Lynne asked in a careful tone.

"I just want to talk."

Lynne barely paused and wrote on the bottom of the goals sheet. Handing it back to me, she asked, "Does this look like what you are hoping for?"

She had written, "Nancy wants to be heard and have her feelings validated."

The flood of relief poured down my face all the way home.

4-28

Staring in a daze up at earnest faces peering back at me over the edge of the cliff, slowly I feel my limbs and stretch my neck checking for injuries. Surprised at still being in this place, shocked at being alive, I reluctantly sit up cautiously observing my surroundings. People at the top are shouting at me to climb back up the cliff. My mind is slow, senses numbed. Heaviness wraps itself over my shoulders like a familiar stole.

Some shouts are scolding and angry. Others are impatient or afraid. In a little while, I manage to crawl my way to the base to witness the height up close. Looking straight up the side of the rock wall and pondering a climb without any ropes or safety apparatus, I sigh in despair. Had not I just said I was too tired to climb any more hills? Is not that why I jumped, to put an end to navigating this endless terrain?

Nevertheless, here I am at the bottom again expected to start over with only the voices to pull me along. I do not want to do it. The cries multiply as more would-be rescuers reject my hesitation. God is up there too, telling me to come. Fear of displeasing him is my motivation. Aching, my hands reach for leverage. Feet and fingers discover crevices in the stone wall as I begin my tedious rise.

If I look down, all the voices scold, "Focus!" Sensing a powerful need for someone to understand why I jumped in the first place, my own shouts rise above the din. Yet only for a moment do unhearing listeners pause.

"Challenge those negative thoughts," they cry.

"I'm weary." My throat cracks.

"Get control of your emotions and stay in the present!" Apparently, the small crowd is assuming I want to be back at the top. I realize it must appear I did not really intend to die or else I would have.

Every time my fingers press into a cleft to lift me a little, the smiling chorus repeats, "Good job! Keep up the positive thinking!" They do not seem to understand I wish to let go, that my passion is steadfast. I am only moving up because I fear God's disappointment. All I have left is God and I cannot afford to lose him.

My slowness is difficult for some to watch while others feel any progress is a sign I do not need them to stay near. Few remain to have their say. I promised I would not jump again—that I would keep climbing. I made that promise in order to be good, to be the proper daughter of a mighty and Holy God who expects so much even as he loves his child deeply. No one has asked why I am climbing or if I even want to.

I am acutely aware it is a simple matter of letting go to achieve promising death. This time I would not make the same mistakes that led to my survival. The voices are growing quiet. I question whether God would really punish me if I quit. Those that are still watching see my hands and feet progressing between the jagged rocks and are pleased. They use words like, "brave" and "strong" in describing my ascent as I smile feebly in their direction so they will not notice the truth. What they do not see is my grip weakening, my will melting away. I lift one finger at a time, flirting with the desire to fall.

Refocusing on Life outside the Tomb

5-15

Upon the final meeting with my hospital psychiatrist, I accepted a challenge to come up with three reasons why it is good to be alive. These many months later that list remains empty. There is a reason *for* staying alive however—-my sons would blame and never forgive themselves. And they would carry that all their lives. The inheritance I would pass on would be that of sadness, hurt, and possibly generational suicide.

Today I wrote out a list of twelve values and actions I can do to bring me to a point where those values are displayed regularly in my life. The first one is honoring God. Primarily right now, that means proactively focusing on living and doing therapy homework. Another value is showing love to Jerry, which at this point in time can be accomplished in a small way by keeping the apartment clean and dinner timely. Being a friend, and becoming a better artist are also important to me. Depression is an excruciating force, and disabling accusations ceaselessly run through my mind. Basing daily to-do lists on these values is keeping me busily distracted.

This negative inner voice has never been easily suspended.

"Mom, the music is too loud!" my teenage sons used to complain.

"I'm supposed to be saying that to you." I would laugh.

"Yeah, well, you're busting our ears. You always play it too loud. Especially in the car."

It is true; music blares in the vehicle much of the time. One afternoon several years ago, pulling up to an intersection, I slowed to see an ambulance barreling in my direction. Punching the gas pedal, an accident was barely averted. Why had not I known an emergency vehicle was nearby? The sirens could not pierce through the volume of the car radio.

There is a simple explanation. That screaming, malicious inner voice cannot be drowned out by normal sound levels.

6-11

Dr. Jay has contacted me following a short series of recent emails going back and forth between us. This time, he has something to say that dumbfounds and leaves me literally speechless.

> Hi Nancy,
>
> I just thought of something. Since you are such a good writer, perhaps you could write something about how once you started to trust the process in IOP and continued it in working with Lynne, you have turned your life around. I would be honored to share it with new clients coming into IOP. You could be an inspiration to so many!! Think about it and let me know.

A resounding *yes*! That is how I have lived my life. I used to call it my reason to get out of bed in the morning, trying to make a difference in the lives of others. This is what my work has been in the past; this is why I am writing now. God's funny, is he not?

6-14

Changing Direction. My experience in IOP, briefly tells the story of my journey so far. It ends with the following paragraphs.

> IOP is three months behind me now. A familiar question confronted me this morning—will I choose to live well? The cycle I feared is still a possibility, and today I wanted to worry, and experience the comfort of isolation while dwelling in my own head. Yearning for relief by means of long-established, self-destructive

measures was causing torment. Glancing at the list of newly defined values and goals laying open beside the couch, I knew it was my choice to either control the intensity of these feelings or give in to them. Knowing how to escape their pull offered some options to this tug-of-war.

For example, honoring my word to God who loves me and to significant persons in my life means I must do the exact opposite of what I feel like doing. I wanted to obsess, so I focused on accomplishing something positive by working on this article. Hiding was tempting, so I contacted a friend. Releasing long-held secrets from their deep reserve is terrifying, thus I made myself share openly with my new therapist. In answer to the draw of self-punishing habits, my hands and mind were kept busy with creating a collage.

These choices accomplished what IOP promised they would—I feel better at the end of the day. Positive distractions not only gave my mind a rest from unsettling emotions, they came with a sense of success. I won this round. Victories like this one may become more and more frequent. Because despondency is most severe in the quiet of night, staying busy throughout the day also helps me to fall asleep more quickly and spares me some difficulty.

Apparently, this CBT stuff works. Despite my attitude, feelings, and doubts, what I have been taught is true. It is by practicing the process that change comes.

Brought to an Abrupt Halt

6-29

Knowing the truth will set you free, but first it may punch you in the gut. Bad news is knocking the air out of me today. This morning I found out I need a biopsy, with cancer being a distinct possibility. Later, Lynne tosses about the term "abuse" some more, and she is certain she is using it correctly with regard to my childhood and marriage. Hearing that experiences can be named as a legitimate cause for my current struggles, has me in shock.

Suddenly my worldview is being challenged. Excuses bathing the misconduct of others are being threatened. In some ways, it hurts to learn they do not work anymore. This afternoon, Jerry called from Colorado where he is on a business trip. In light of the fact we have not used the term, he surprised me with the "A" word.

"I'm sorry I've been abusive to you. I am so sorry I have been immature and hurtful in our relationship. It hurts me to think I have hurt you. I want to change. Please forgive me."

I am floored and somewhat pleased, but doubt he knows all he is admitting. As he continues by disclosing past sins against me with his own version of excuses, I realize I am right.

6-30

The biopsy is scheduled for Tuesday with pre-op testing today. I have doubts about following through. Why would I want to know if I have cancer or not? If there is none, then not knowing does not matter. If cancer is present and I am told about it, a choice will have to be made. Of all years, why would I want to face a life or death cancer question now? Nine years ago, when my mother and mother-in-law died of cancer I swore I would not fight it if it happened to me.

Bottom line is I do not value living at all costs. However, if my decision is not to pursue treatment at present, my sons might not understand. People may believe I chose to let cancer run its course for suicidal reasons. Besides, they might be partially correct.

Still, the phone call is made, cancelling both appointments.

7-1

Any positive feedback I have received from readers of my written works is like food for my spirit. Famished for encouragement, I read their responses repeatedly. When an email from Jerry showed up in my inbox a few days ago, all the others went to the sidelines. His opinion matters that much to me.

> Dearest Nancy,
>
> Yes, I see a lot about you in the magazine article you forwarded to me. About both of us. And I think we are both at the point where we need to accept ourselves as we are, then as God sees us.
>
> That is why it is so important for you to write. You could help so many by sharing your experience. You are wonderful, dear. I pray for you as you struggle through each day that God will keep you and work in your life in the midst of what you feel. Especially, that he will use this to bless the socks off others and help them.
>
> Jerry

The many years Jerry rarely spoke to me except for basic necessary communication, nearly destroyed what self-esteem lingered. If I could express the acuteness of my loneliness at that time, it would probably surprise people who knew me back then. There were days I thought about leaving the marriage, but where would I go? I would be alone with a divorce and two unhappy children added to the mix.

My daily striving was centered on pleasing a man who would not be pleased. It took as many as three to four hours each week to prepare a grocery list as I agonized over what meals would make him happy. Each afternoon was tense as I fretted over what to cook. Ultimately, it did not matter as each dinner had something wrong with it. The house was not clean enough; I was spending "his" money. If I asked for help with household chores, even while the boys were toddlers, he would refuse by adding that he had put in his eight hours and was done for the day. My maid status exasperated me as I cleaned up his piles of clutter, laundry, and dirt. A few years into our marriage, I actually sent him a bill "for services rendered." It made me chuckle, but did nothing to change the situation or emit appreciation from him.

Food service, alterations, and retail jobs I took outside the home were not ones I wanted. Even a position as Director of Children's Church was one to meet his standards of value. I had to bring home some of the bacon.

Blame, public hushing, and "you embarrass me" comments deeply hurt. Being ignored threatened to break me. For about eight years, especially as he struggled with his own Major Depression, he would return home from work, walk past me, greet our dog and pet him enthusiastically, then retreat to the TV for the evening. I did not get as much acknowledgement as the dog. One afternoon during our twenty-fourth year as husband and wife, he admitted he did not love me and had not for ten years.

I compare my reaction to our relationship to how I heard mice would act in one experiment. They are placed in a box with food at one end. At first the rodents are free to roam as they wish, eat when they want. Then an electrical current is applied crossing the path to their meal. Sometimes it is turned on and often is not. Still, the mice will venture to the area where the current threatens, and risk pain for the food on the other side. The electricity begins to flow more frequently, yet still they cross the line. Even after pain has become a guarantee and the food is permanently removed, these critters will return, then again, to face the consequences of their efforts at satisfying their hunger.

An emotionally destructive relationship offers fulfillment in its early stages. Long after the once unpredictable stings have become a regular feature, the emotionally starved partner will continue to seek that original reward which may infrequently or never come.

It is understandable then I am hesitant to trust his affirmative words now. Back to the old expectation of a second dropping shoe, it seems this is one more lesson to unlearn. Like a wise little mouse, I will sit back to watch and wait.

7-2

Major Depression is tough. Recovery is painfully slow. One day I am more energetic and the next I have nothing left. Today, I am wiped out. Seeing Lynne is the only reason I got out of bed, even though there is cleaning to do before our oldest son, Jon, comes to visit tomorrow. So far, I have done little to prepare, barely able to move in the last three days. This morning I forced myself to vacuum and pulled the carpet shampooer out of the closet.

"You got hit with some pretty big stuff this week on multiple levels. It takes a lot of energy to talk about the things we are talking about," Lynne says.

"As we prepared to return from our last visit to Ohio, Jon said to me, 'I don't know what I will do when you are gone. I don't mean when you are gone to Philly. Right now, I can call you, but I can't dial 1-800-heaven.'" I smile as I relate the story.

"That's very sweet! The main reason people stop themselves from suicide is because of the people they will leave behind." Lynne cautions, "Your sons will be impacted for the rest of their lives."

It is hard to remember that suicide is off the table. At least I told Dr. Jay I think it is. That is how it has stayed—a thought of maybe. This secret death wish has pervaded my thoughts for a long time. It has been suggested maybe some of this is habit.

Lynne recommends I write myself a warning letter to be read when depressed. "Don't do it. This will destroy your sons!" Making the quality decision, "I will not commit suicide," means being willing to go to the Emergency Room if those thoughts come, to try and make suicide an anathema to me.

"The thinking of people who attempt suicide is cloudy, I know, and in compassion I understand the emotional anguish is great. You now clearly know it was not God's voice leading you to attempt suicide?" Lynne pursues the months-old question.

"I think I am. There are lingering doubts."

"I want you to reach the place where you are one hundred percent certain this is not of God." Her eyes focus on my face. "Nancy, you are telling me horrible stories but show no affect. It's like you are reading out of a newspaper. I'm not sensing any feelings from you."

"I believe I'm not allowed to express them. Especially sad ones," I reply.

"Take that to scripture," Lynne urges. "What does God say?"

This brings a story to remembrance. Grinnell, Kansas, has a population of four hundred. At least that was the case the year we lived there—1984. Downtown sported a post office and a grocery market. It was while on a shopping excursion there that I met Andy. He looked pitiful and hungry. My heart went out to him and I tried to approach. As the distance closed between us, he turned and hobbled away as fast as his three good and one possibly broken leg would carry him. Obviously, he did not get far. Purchasing groceries as quickly as possible, I added a bag of dog food, hoping he would still be outside when the transaction was complete.

He was. Crawling up to anyone who came near, he was searching for something to eat. He was a Blue Heeler, I guessed to be around six-months-old. There was no way he was going to let me carry him, so dropping some food on the sidewalk, I stepped back to watch. It was gone in a blink. He was so hungry, I almost cried.

It was a short walk home I was so excited that he was following me. As I turned to enter the adjoining garage, food in hand, Andy took off. As he was yet unnamed, I called out in a panic, "Puppy! Come here, boy." He hesitated and I knelt, coaxing, "It's okay, you are safe here. C'mon, you can do it!"

Slowly he slunk across the yard and cautiously came to where I had laid out the food. From that point, he was mine.

He had been abused, that much was certain. Bruises along with the injured leg could have been from a terrible accident. However, it was his fear; his nearly paralyzed manner of approaching that told me what he had suffered.

Somehow, in a manner I do not remember, he ended up in our living room. He would not leave the corner where he stared at the wall, hunched over as if expecting the boot. He wound up on a blanket alongside food and water, and that is where he stayed.

For two whole days.

Traumatized Andy barely moved. It required hours of sitting with him, talking, and petting him to retrieve any spirit in the damaged dog. His physical healing resolved rather quickly as his leg was apparently not broken after all. By the time he grew the courage to leave the blanket behind, he was walking straight and no longer limping.

He and I became inseparable. He was a refuge for my heart as surely as I was helping him. My injuries, a poor and broken spirit, have me limping through life, hiding from intimacy, from being real. If I could stay curled up on a blanket in a corner somewhere and never come out, maybe I would.

Andy. A joy to be sure. It broke my heart when one year later, in ignorant confidence, he ran in front of a car and died on the spot.

7-10

Comments directed at me over the years have included: "You are open to a point, and then no one can cross that line;" "You have a way of saying things that make them seem less important than they are;" "All the years I have known you, I have perceived you as strong and very independent and 'aloof'. In control." "There was this distance or wall that just did not let people in. If you were suffering back in those years we were spending time together, there was no indication of it. My perception was that you were unapproachable. Above all the rest of us. Cold."

The years to which these comments refer were some of the most agonizing of my life. Since some things are better left unsaid, and because of my husband's ministry role, I did not think people should know I hurt. Tremendous fear of annoying others has also closed my lips thousands of times. Well-constructed masks and costumes rarely fail in their primary purpose of rendering the wearer unrecognizable. The most desired ones in fantasy and mystery tales achieve invisibility. Somehow, it appears mine was effective.

Twenty-two years ago I was told, "You are difficult to love." This not being my intention of course, the idea was nearly dismissed. It was not me making relationships hard, but it was the unseeing, unhearing people who did not understand or care.

Nonetheless, could I be unlovable? The question strikes at my core. Actually, it would not surprise me that much if it were true. It is not an unfamiliar fear, which today sends me back into the shadows.

Learning to Lean

7-12

As long as busyness holds my attention, overwhelming emotions remain in the background. However, like a dog on a chain, they make much noise and try to break loose. With any temporary halt in activity, I feel like I could fall off an edge into a pit. In spare moments I tear up. During longer gaps between projects, the sobbing starts. Last night a pleasant phone call made me feel good. Nevertheless, once off the call, my thoughts were, "Man, this life sucks. I'm lonely." All it takes is a brief pause for sorrow and anger to take over.

I am not sure what the gloom is about. It is difficult being in my head, with bad memories, and picturing them. Regrets pop up and will not leave me alone.

History has been secreted away for so long it has come out in dreams, and now is leaking through my face.

7-13

"Maybe you need to return to IOP," Lynne said. "My concern is once there you would hide."

"Yeah, I might."

"It seems you are so used to not putting your feelings into words that you think you will be overwhelmed. When someone is six months on suicide watch, the therapist may not be looking so hard at all the other issues. You bring up what you need to talk about," she said.

"What I'm feeling is more of an ambivalence. Should I go to IOP and work on expressing emotions? I wonder if it would be best to remain as I am.

"Because life can be hard. Your life has been hard. I am hoping that ambivalence inside of you includes hope that you can enjoy life. You are changing your self-image. Even for a positive, it is scary." Lynne smiled reassuringly.

Later that afternoon, a round of emails opened the door to giving IOP another try.

> Hi Dr. Jay,
>
> Lynne and I are discussing sending me back to IOP. Before a decision can be made, I need to ask you a question, if you don't mind. Would it

be possible to refrain from giving out my story while I am attending IOP?

> Thanks,
> Nancy

Sure. When are you thinking of returning?

> Dr. Jay

As soon as possible.

> Nancy

Let's plan for Monday. I am out of the office this week.

> Dr. Jay

7-16

Shot in the feet. That is what Jerry and I are as a couple, and we have done it to ourselves. Withdrawing from society, not attending church, or reaching our hands of friendship toward anyone else for months has left us emotionally crippled. It is time to learn to walk again.

Tomorrow we join a Sunday School class of people our age. The grapevine informed us they are friendly there. Right now, I do not know how I will get through greeting new faces or shaking hands. But I will. I always do. I will manage with smiles and a cheerful demeanor all the while a corkscrew is turning in my stomach and a verbal onslaught worthy of ice pick status strikes inside my skull. After it is over, I will disintegrate.

7-19

I am gaining the new perspective that wrong has been done to me in contrast with supposing I have received what I deserve. Moreover, I am being exposed to the idea that emotional pain is a legitimate response. My new tentative goals are admitting to others that I feel pain at deep levels, overcoming the automatic shut-off that occurs when dealing with pain, and forgiving myself for anything I think I did to cause problems or distress to anyone including myself. Wow, what a thought! IOP may be the place I need to experiment with stepping out and admitting what I feel to other people.

"You are taking care of yourself, which is new in some ways," Dr. Jay says cheerfully.

"Yes. My moods are all over the place," I say. "Sometimes they can just go to hell and back. Last Saturday night the thought came to me, *You could always just kill yourself.* Then after twenty minutes of thinking about how I could accomplish that, I took that thought to task. *No, this is not what God wants. Just stop.* So I stopped the suicidal thinking."

"That's a very different process you were doing this time. That's a testament to you." He smiles. "It has worked out ideally for you to be here now.

Circumstances kept me from handing out your story in the last two weeks. So everybody who is in group now hasn't read it."

"Much time and energy and anxiety was spent on whether I should show up today. I had been asking God, 'Please tell me if I should go or not'. To find out you have not handed out my story for two weeks is proof to me he was actually preparing the way for me to come back here. He keeps doing things like that."

Agreeing, Dr. Jay nods. "It's amazing when we start paying attention how many times he actually visits."

As IOP group members share their stories, Dr. Jay is teaching us that the missing, vital step toward healing is validation. When I see a tragic story on the news and the reporter makes an emotional comment, or if it is announced that counselors are being made available to victims' friends and families, my initial reaction is surprise. It seems a wonder to me that it is okay for those people to feel something, that sadness is openly talked about, and that the world approves of them feeling and talking about it. As old as I am, it still gives me pause.

This goes back to my core beliefs unearthed months ago that feelings equal weakness, and it is shameful to expose the deep or sad ones. In reality, feelings are not to be judged, they just are. No one has control over what feelings come up. Neither can any of us stop thoughts from entering our minds. Life just hits each of us.

A goal might be to look at how I am reacting and perhaps decide to change that reaction. What kind of person do I want to be? What do I need to do or think about to become that person?

"Everyone has been told in one form or another, 'You did that wrong,'" Dr. Jay says. "What if those messages were incorrect? That totally changes everything, doesn't it?"

7-21

"Lynne is telling me it is not selfish to try and get my needs met, yet at church and in Christian books I am hearing we are supposed to be other-oriented." Several people are gathered in the IOP circle today. "How can it be okay for me to be focusing all this energy, time, and money on myself, when God's way is supposed to come first? Isn't it God's job to meet my basic needs while I concentrate on loving other people?"

A woman answers, "It would be hard to be there for other people when your own needs are not met."

"I agree, it is just that in any situation God can be the one to meet my needs."

"You need to take this time to gain understanding so he can use you in the future. Then you will be able to say with confidence to someone else who is suicidal, 'It's okay. You'll come through to the other side,'" she says.

Dr. Jay adds, "Nancy, this confusion has a familiar quality. Knowing some of your background, I think this may be coming from the sense that you are not important, not worth much. If you are holding on to the belief, 'I'm not valuable,' then the corresponding idea that you are not supposed to take care of your own needs can be covered in part by saying 'I'm going to let God do that.'"

What if I could trust that God-given gut instinct that tells me I am sad, I am hurt, I need support. It would be something to grant myself permission to reach out, to allow someone to be here for me. Maybe that attacking voice of guilt could even be silenced.

What if?

7-24

Tough. One of the reasons I think I ignore red flags is because I think I can easily either fix or handle the problem. Then I put off getting help in all kinds of situations because it is a sign of weakness to ask. Realizing a few years back that I am not tough was difficult news to take. Nevertheless, I can still pretend I am.

People praise strength as a virtue. An individual who has a strong back, can take *it* without buckling, knows how not to get hurt by words, and never complains while in physical pain, is admired. Toughness in my interpretation is the ability not to be bent over by life's pressures. It is holding one's head high, beating the odds, being a conqueror. That is not me.

Perhaps toughness is just what the so-called strong put forward. What if pretending to be strong is a normal way of life for everyone? Groups like IOP present the truth; the not so tough are not alone.

In my thinking, if my strength is not across the board, then I am altogether weak. The question has been posed to me; can I be somewhat strong, or strong in one area and weak in another?

Could it be okay not only to be weak, but also to allow it to be seen? Is that what is called, "being human?"

7-26

"Sometimes I feel I really want to embrace the positive," a group member mentions.

Dr. Jay warns him saying, "It's a fine line. When a bad thing happens to us, it's good to feel badly about it because that tells us what we experienced is real and matters." Then he added something surprising to me. "I've never seen anyone really make progress without the first step of validation."

"Realizing that what happened is important?" I ask.

"Yes. Without that we can't move forward."

So, that is what was going on back in June! When Lynne identified what had happened in my past in psychological terms, she was validating my experiences. She was opening my eyes to the fact that what I had felt all these years was legitimate—that what happened was important.

Validation is missing when people do not want to get it, or do not agree. Such as the woman who told me she does not believe depression is a disease. Others do get it and support me, while some expect recovery to be accomplished in a short while.

How do I need supportive people to show up for me? What I need most is non-judgmental presence: a note, an email, a call, a visit, a Facebook comment. These things are like air and water to me. When they do not come, the inner voice does. I tend to feel uncared for in silence. Loneliness consumes me in solitude.

8-4

"What's the test you have tomorrow?" Dr. Jay asks.

"Pre-op for a biopsy. I have been putting this off for a month. It brings up a lot of...it's confusing. I mean, seven months ago I wanted to die more than anything else, right? So now there's this possibility of a terminal disease, and I've done all this emotional work for nothing."

"Whew. Black and white thinking again," he says as he catches my wording.

I am oblivious. "Is it? Seems logical to me."

"Nancy, that assumes you are not better off now than you were seven months ago."

I am bi-lingual. I speak both black and white fluently. As Lynne and Dr. Jay repeatedly point out "gray" concepts, I imagine my brain is operated by hamsters running feverishly on spinning wheels. To one side is a large black wheel. Another large wheel on the opposite side is white. The faster the creatures on those two wheels move their little feet (and they can move them very fast), the more eloquently I speak my two languages.

In the middle is situated a miniscule gray wheel. Its lethargic, tiny hamster weakly staggers inside, causing the squeak to be barely audible. It is pathetic.

Black and white thinking is pervasive in my mind, speech, and behaviors. It affects my decisions, perceptions, and outlook. It has held me back from spiritual and emotional growth, and has even affected my physical health. Most areas of my life, especially on the relationship level, have been adversely affected by black and white thinking.

Learning to speak gray will require language school. Recognizing that I think in extremes, I have been trying to get rid of words like all, always, never, and replacing should with could. In reality, life is fuller of gray language than either black or white.

Now if I could just get my hamsters to cooperate.

8-6

I may have turned a corner recently. I am hesitant to say that because typically, terrible moods follow good ones. Lynne suggested I am applying black and white thinking to my mental health—that if a good mood turns sour, it was never actually good. That if I feel good, I have to remain that way, or else I failed to be well.

The first two weeks of this round of IOP I thought were maybe making me worse, but therapy can open wounds before it heals them, so I did not quit. Non-patronizing care from Dr. Jay and Lynne has been eye opening. If for no other reason, I thank God he brought us to Pennsylvania for the quality of mental health care we are finding here.

Stumbling in the Right Direction

8-8

"I am overwhelmed by all the changes made and to be made yet. When Lynne put a name to my experiences, when you responded to one of my stories with 'Shocking!,' I can't even tell you what that meant to me. I couldn't believe it." I am addressing Dr. Jay. We and the rest of the IOP group are gathered in a warm office during a record-breaking heat wave.

"So, you've been hearing validation from a number of people." Dr. Jay looks pleased.

"Yes. I did not know I live in a world of black and white. But I do. I am beginning to see it as it happens. Jerry is starting to see how he thinks in black and white also, and our views clash. That is when it got to feeling overwhelming, when we realized two fifty-year-old people have to change their entire worldviews. It is too much. I am not sure we can do it. He cried when he said, 'How is it that we have lived so many years and are just now learning this?' We are both frustrated about that. And of course, I feel it has to be resolved right now!"

"That's extreme thinking." A group member laughs.

"Yes! I know." Then smiling, I say, "And the woulda-couldas are a waste of time."

"It can also be validating to go back and find out why this hasn't been learned before now," Dr. Jay suggests.

"And it's not like I didn't try." Recalling failed attempts at finding kind and competent therapists, I add, "I just haven't had the information before."

Dr. Jay is encouraging. "You are seeing it now. And you are moving forward."

Initially I misunderstood CBT in light of my need to vent. However, it is helping in adjusting my thought processes. By any measure, the most difficult CBT directive for me has been challenging negative core beliefs by searching for evidence to the contrary.

For example, my belief that God has been disappointed in me this year is contrasted with who he has been throughout all my years and what the Bible says about him. The evidence for his patience with me is obvious; Jesus has not ceased calling. Regardless of any shift in my mood, he has continued to show up, guide my steps, and open my mind to new promising ideas.

He uses his children's struggles to teach us, to sand down the rough spots in our wooden heads! Still, he has set no time limit on our learning.

··•●•··

My biopsy came back normal. No cancer. Most people would find my reaction to the news strange, the lack of relief. Obviously, my state of mind needs more healing. Each time in IOP, I am confronted with the fear of letting people in, exposing my true self. The old belief that expressing emotions will annoy people needs to be met head-on. Every day, I face Jerry with distrust and drag my feet on following through with marriage counseling homework. The threat of being left alone must cease controlling me.

None of this is easy. In fact, it is all painful. Nonetheless, my choices are most often to behave in a different way than I feel like acting, staying away from suicidal thoughts, speaking up in group, and continuing in my marriage.

That is what CBT has taught me to do. My walking out of the tomb has so far been slow and tedious, rife with indecision and close calls. I may be stumbling, but at least it is toward the exit. Despite how I feel.

8-9

Three events have to take place in order for a thought to become a belief. Both external and internal reinforcements have to occur.

"To begin, it has to be told to you," Dr. Jay has said. "Next, experience has to show it to you. Finally, the thought has to be repeated by you."

If my belief is that affirmations are followed by great pain, someone must have spoken those words or in some way strongly transmitted that message to me, in this case during childhood. Reinforcement of that idea comes in the form of disappointing relationships and my interpretation of those scenarios. For example, when my first boss fired me a few weeks after having enthusiastically hiring me, the thought that pain follows affirmation was supported. Negative self-talk has since strongly cemented that thought as a belief.

If any one of these elements is missing, the thought will remain just a thought. When a belief already exists, change comes hard. Positive evidence that disproves it has to be deliberately searched out, and earnestly considered. Speaking reinforcement of the negative belief to oneself has to stop.

The injurious voice in my head once belonged to significant people in my life. Repeatedly, its message has been poured into my thoughts, and my heart. It is seeping throughout my being; my fight is a sieve against a river. Over time, no one can know precisely when, without my awareness it had morphed into something other than what I heard and became what I believed. Sometime along, the brutal voice became my own.

8-12

We talk about compulsions, the "I have to do this" kind of urge. Dr. Jay suggests it would help to have the opposing argument up where it can be seen. Then it becomes our choice to follow through on the undesirable behavior or to read the list. The black and white thinking he wants to hear from the group is our decisions that suicide is off the table, and that we have said, "I won't consider it anymore."

Today I sit at the computer searching the internet for stories written by loved ones of those who have killed themselves. My motive is to gather tears from the eyes of children who have lost their mothers and collect their sobs in my arms. I need this information so I will not forget the heart wrenching I could bestow on my sons if I were to follow through with suicidal thoughts. The World Wide Web does not have many secrets; nonetheless, I am stunned at the sheer number of posted messages from family survivors.

No message is hopeful. All are drenched in sorrow and one common question, "Why?" I read recently written letters to the dead by sons and daughters whose parent died decades ago. Grandchildren who never knew their ancestor write of their unrealized dreams of relationship. The truth unfolds before me in the glaring light of my monitor. No one actually *survives* a completed suicide. The hearts of surrounding persons die along with the body of the despairing.

Despite several additions, my Mental Health Wall has plenty of space on it. I copy some of those messages, especially the ones that prove time does not heal this kind of wound, and hang them up. Clearly, the damage done to my sons would be disastrous. I write:

> I broke the legacy of divorce, violence, screaming matches, and unanswered questions. What legacy will I be passing on to generations to come if I kill myself?

The Legacy of Suicide

Statistics suggest suicide is hereditary. Those closest to the dead are at the highest risk for suicide than any other group.

Personal values and beliefs of those left behind are shattered.

Friends and family are changed emotionally.

Suicide forms a precedent for others to follow by giving rise to an acceptable option.

My Legacy

Every kid asks, "Does what my parents taught me stand even when I test it?" I have taught Jon and Tim to keep their eyes on Jesus, to choose his reality over what they see in the world around them. What would my suicide be teaching them about faith? What could they possibly infer about Christ if their mother gave up?

Most people who make decisions about God do so in relation to one of life's challenges. Even my death by natural means would be a huge change for my sons. What would they decide about all I have poured into their hearts if their spiritually defining life challenge is my suicide?

When I die, their question will be "Why?" If I die of natural causes, this will be automatically directed at God. He is able to satisfy them.

However, in the event of my suicide, their question would be directed at me, and I will not be able to answer.

STEADY NOW, "JUST WALK"

8-16

"You always beat yourself up, Nancy." The group is looking at me as Dr. Jay proceeds. "How would it feel to not have guilt? What would it take?"

"I don't know," I answer shrugging my shoulders. "It's like breathing. In every relationship, every social situation, I always believe I have done something wrong. When people about me seem unhappy, it is my fault. If I did not cause their discomfort, I am failing to fix it. Even walking away from IOP I feel like I shouldn't have said what I did, acted inappropriately, or hurt others somehow."

Dr. Jay is sympathetic. "I'm sorry you feel that way. That is really painful. I'm sorry you suffer like that." He pauses. "Is there any room for forgiveness? Doesn't God know we are human?"

"I feel there are things I do that don't please him."

"Does it please God that you feel guilty all the time?"

"I am harder on myself than God is. God loves me and understands. Yeah, I'm harder on myself," I say.

Conversation moves on to another group member who backslid into destructive habits over the past weekend. After a few minutes, he is asked if he wants to get well. Then Dr. Jay turns to me and says, "I want you to think about this too, Nancy."

"For me, getting well means I will wind up staying alive. As I feel better, there is a growing sense of urgency. *Kill yourself now before it is too late.* I am trying to come up with reasons not to do it, but at the moment, I can rationalize toying with the thought. Jon recently asked me about our family medical history, and I mentioned that on my side people tend to go downhill fast after age seventy. I told him I do not want to live past seventy for that reason, then asked how that makes him feel. He said it makes him feel bad because it sounds as if I do not want to be here, and he still needs me."

"Write that down!" The group agrees with Dr. Jay.

"I will. I need that reason to stay alive. When I look toward the future I see things that are coming, things I don't want."

A man confesses his fear of losing friends if he gets well because they have rallied around him during this time. Dr. Jay asks me, "Can you relate to that?"

I shake my head. "It's been kind of the opposite for me. Oh, happy Nancy isn't here anymore and so let's scoot."

Ever the one to sneak up on me with gray ideas, Dr. Jay questions, "Is that a reason to get better?"

Sighing, I answer. "I don't know. Have to think about it."

8-18

"Ha-ha! Keep walking!" Jerry was encouraging.

Laughing, I hollered, "I am trying! Ahhhh!" Gripping the too-wide wooden rails, my fingertips ached.

"Don't look at the floor," Jerry suggested in earnest. "Look straight ahead."

Balance was tenuous in that Fun House. A slat floor on bearings slid beneath my feet, and each step threatened to send me kaput.

I do not remember how old we were; it was a long time ago. Yet it is still funny to remember that crazy floor. Focusing on progress up the continuum is an ordeal of balance as well. Being wobbly, uncertain, and tense, looking straight ahead is simple until the next motion shifts the ground underneath into a mad roll. Focusing on positive possibilities is not a cure for depression, but it keeps one moving forward.

Nancy,

Past influences play a role and you can choose to give some weight or a lot of weight to them. What if you gave more value to what you are experiencing now in IOP with the relationships you have there and with Lynne and me? Use your current experiences to guide your trust and belief in being able to change what you want. What if you focused on those relationships and what you are getting from them (e.g. understanding, support, encouragement, honesty, feedback, opportunities to help others, making others smile, feeling safe to be vulnerable, etc.)? What if...?

Dr. Jay

Somehow, the dirt floor in this tomb quivers as much as the silly one in the Fun House. There are no rails here, and of course, my hands and feet are still bound. This precarious situation is familiar. As old as I am, and as barely resurrected, I still fully expect a figurative swooping backhand to appear from nowhere and send me flying. I am tensed, awaiting the wind to be knocked out of me.

I shared my list of negative core beliefs with Dr. Jay, along with some positive ones I insisted could not be challenged. He said, "They can be challenged if you do not believe them." I know this man who has been nothing but kind to me was just suggesting a perspective. Nevertheless, I read anger in his face, and heard, "Your stupidity annoys me. Try something else, you dumb nuisance. When are you going to stop coming here and bothering the rest of us?"

What if this thinking could change? Lynne and Dr. Jay are assuring me it can. How can I explain what it is like to be more certain of upcoming harm than of my next breath? The chair I am sitting on feels sturdy, has held me for years, and I have no doubt it will still be holding me five minutes from now. Not so with love and value. It is conceivable to me that in the next five minutes anyone who has cared for me could stop doing so. It is perfectly conceivable that they already have.

8-19

It is disappointing when friends back-off, especially when desperation is so intense. Yet that may be the very reason they run. Dr. Jay asks me what I said recently to bring Rose to request I leave her alone for a few weeks. She and I share knowledge and personal experience with Major Depression. I thought it was safe the other day to tell her when my self-destructive thoughts had evolved into reckless behavior. Instead, she suggested I tell someone else in charge of my care.

Her words "need a break" are akin to dismissal in my understanding. In actuality, Rose has her own mental health to take care of and said as much. Dr. Jay suggests some choices of words can heighten fear in listeners. Perhaps I could say, "I feel hopeless" instead of "I want to die."

This feeds right into my literal and precise use of words. "Hopeless" to me means without hope. At all. None. Since I obviously feel some hope that a conversation will relieve a bit of the pressure, (or else why would I be contacting anyone) then I am definitively not feeling hopeless. I do however, want to die. It is going to be a learning process, figuring out how to approach communication in a less literal way. I am wondering how on earth this learning is going to take place. Trial and error has not worked well for fifty years.

As for the case of Rose, who has been encouraging and patient for months, Dr. Jay asked me to imagine he and I are playing catch in the back yard. If he lobs the ball my way and I catch it then toss it back, we are having a game. However, if the ball comes my way and I just stand there, he may fetch it and try to throw it again to me. How long would I expect him to keep trying? Relative to my friends, if in the context of their support and advice I do not seem to participate, they may quit.

Lynne reminds me in this light; it is necessary to get across to friends and supports what I need in the moment instead of expecting them to know. Alternatively, if I tell them once, plan to have to say it again later. Obviously, their world does not revolve around me and so giving them some grace to forget, be too busy, misunderstand, not relate, have unrealistic expectations, be tired, be stressed, be overburdened, be scared, or to need a break is warranted. I am my own responsibility, after all.

Another consideration is whom am I inviting into my life? Am I sometimes choosing friends who will not respond or at least not in a positive way? My background's mix of emotional neglect and trauma leads to the question whether my selection of persons for friendship is fed by the innate sense of low worth.

If I do not deserve to be valued, then safe friends who will value me will be left off the list.

According to my therapists, it is okay to test friendships. Not only is it okay, it is necessary. In addition, one person may be safe at one point and then not so later because their circumstances changed. There are no guarantees. Nevertheless, I do not need to neglect my needs in selecting friends, and do not have to be so hard on them, either.

8-20

Today is not like before. I have had some strong thoughts that I would never commit suicide, however there has been much fear mixed in. This day is different because, my thought is not only, *I should take suicide off the table*, but also, *I sort of want to*.

8-21

"You have a strong knowledge of how to stop old behaviors, want to stop these behaviors, and yet there continues a strong pull to carry them out. How can you get to a Regis Philbin-style *final* decision?" Dr. Jay asks.

What a great question! This entire year I have been a yo-yo, determined one day to move upward, the next to drop back. I have not given up, demolished, or buried the "escape route" mentality chosen on the day of my suicide attempt. Equally, I have not quit aspiring to honor God. The latter is encouraged by nearly everyone who knows the situation. In my heart, I know I should let this side of the fight win. Lynne says I am feeding the wrong dog.

Months ago, she gave me papers to sign—commitments never to attempt suicide again and to follow a set route of options in the case of crisis. Yet unsigned, the battle continues.

Walking in the near pitch-blackness of night on our country property as a young girl, my imagination created monsters out of tree branches and threats out of shadows. Nevertheless, I knew my fears were getting the best of me, and I determined to walk. Just walk.

Dark shapes grew larger when the wind blew, and scattered their fingers across the gray lawn scratching as if pursuing something, someone. Eerie shades of dusky orange emanated from behind the clouds, granting little relief. Successfully managing to control my steps and not my beating heart, I would whisper to my eager-to-run legs, "Just walk."

Certainly, I knew the trees were not dangerous. Ha! They were just climbing apparatuses and sources of shade! The real question was who was behind those trees? What malicious character lurked in the shadows just waiting for me to get near? Breathing heavily and walking fast, forcing my eyes straight ahead, I would see out of their corners gloomy forms stealthily making their way toward me. I may have been able to walk that path on clear nights, controlling my panic with my whisper. However, if a movement in the trees was at all unusual, that walk was a speedy one. If a dog barked, I was off like a shot.

It is that old fear keeping me from signing those papers. What hides in the murky shadows of the future? I can make out the darkness and sense the threats easily enough. What if one day I need to run out of here?

A dog is barking. I whisper, "Just walk."

8-22

I am thinking about the questions, "What do you want?" and "What if?"

In considering what bit of control I might have over how much suffering comes my way, I have begun to ask what it is I have tried before that did not work, and what have I not tried that might work. An idea has clicked. What if I proactively sought out support instead of waiting for it to come to me? What if?

As for what I honestly want, a list is written:

1. To continue life if happy, to not continue life if sad and lonely
2. To change my black and white thinking in these areas:
    (a) Life can be worth it and include suffering also. (I used to believe this, maybe I can again.)
    (b) I have some control over how much I suffer. Maybe I can improve my health and emotional wellbeing.
    (c) Slipping up on behavioral health goals or even regressing is not the end of all hope.

> (d) People's anger does not mean I have no choices. (I used to be stronger in this area, maybe I can get strong again.)
>
> 3. To trust God to fulfill his purpose in my life no matter my circumstances.
> 4. To allow myself to believe that what I have experienced matters.
> 5. To stop beating myself up constantly. Maybe one minute of peace? Maybe one hour? What if I could experience one whole day of being kind to the hurting little girl curled up inside?

8-23

"She has to be affirmed again and again," Jerry complains to Doug Kaskin, our marriage counselor.

"That's not true," I argue, suspecting it is.

"Do you think Jerry is capable of giving you what you want?" Doug asks.

"One thing I can get caught up in is trying to get all my needs met by Jerry. I know the reality is he cannot achieve that. But he doesn't seem to want to listen to what I need."

"I suggest in order for Jerry to listen he has to be ready to listen," Doug says. "So ask, 'can you listen to me right now?' And wait for him to say yes before continuing."

"Another issue with communication is that I am not necessarily out of judgment mode if he wants to talk about his needs. I may be in fix-it mode," I confess.

"Most men don't like that," he says.

"No, it probably seems like disrespect to him." I hesitate. "Maybe it is disrespect. Jerry and I need to talk about the past. Some of what has gone on in our marriage has traumatized me in the sense I am not getting over it. It still affects who I am today. We also need to talk about the things that have happened that are still affecting who he is today because this has not been a happy marriage, and we are both at fault. We need to learn how to discuss all this."

"That's a great idea," Doug says.

8-30

IOP begins. "We were going to start today with you, Nancy. I can see on your paperwork that you accomplished a lot yesterday. Must have been a good day!"

"It was a tempting, trying day. Especially the morning," I answer, recalling the negative urges and depression of the day before.

"What if you measured it by how much you got done? Would you say then it was a good day?" Dr. Jay is trying to goad me into saying something positive about myself.

"I'd say it was better than the day before."

"There's a tug, isn't there?" He grins. "When is it good enough?"

"I don't know. I was thinking nothing is going to change if I do not get out there and give it a try. So I registered for a Leadership meeting in the Women's

Ministry program at church. If there is a job I can handle, I will sign up for it."

"So if we just look at yesterday, we could say you went pretty far up the continuum activity-wise," he says.

"Yes, and I would modify that to say—"

Now he is laughing along with the rest of the group.

"It's a positive modification!" I smile. "It wasn't just activity; it was activity that leads to somewhere."

"Can you enjoy that you moved up the continuum? You honored not only God, but yourself."

"I didn't see it that way," I answer.

"It's okay to honor you. You have value."

My eyes roll.

"Don't roll your eyes at me!" he scolds humorously.

Playful banter about disrespecting him circles the room.

After a few laughs, he continues. "That's hard for you to hear. What if you were able to actually take that in?"

Hesitating, I try to remember if I have had the experience of honoring me. Nothing comes to mind. Every good memory of success, achievement, and friendship is tinged with guilt. "I don't know what that would be like."

"Or you don't know how to react," a woman adds.

There is general agreement. "A compliment that you had a great day seems foreign to you. You typically dismiss it." Dr. Jay's prodding continues. "It is okay to want to feel good. Do you believe that?" The group is watching me intently during the long pause that follows. "You get stuck there." He smiles.

"Uh huh."

"That's one of those beliefs I would like you to challenge and perhaps change." For now, he has given up his mission. Addressing the group, he asks, "What are you going to work on between now and our next meeting?"

Following various responses, I confess, "Sometimes I will play around with my medications just to mess with my health. I know it's dangerous—"

"Well, it's not suicide, but there's a part of you that struggles with wanting to be healthy," Dr. Jay says.

"Yes. So as for what I need to work on, I have said before I need to be good. Maybe I will add two words to that. Maybe I need to be good to myself?"

"Great!"

8-31

Because of Hurricane Irene's threats to our area, four days ago Jerry had to leave to babysit the computers in the data center at his workplace. I was left alone for twenty-four hours with devastating thoughts that had been hounding me all year, yet had been growing in strength for days. A creeping fear of abandonment had become overpowering. Efforts at contacting a couple people left me talking to voicemails, and no callbacks followed. By Sunday night, I had developed a suicide plan for the third time this year, gathered the means, and had written a suicide note.

Clearly, negative self-talk brought me to that place. Evidence for my beliefs was readily available in memory and recent events. These I chose to focus upon rather than any positive alternatives available to me. Exactly how this intention to commit suicide shifted, I am unsure. Rereading the note struck me with how wounding my last words were to be. I knew they would bring enduring pain to many people. Somehow, my brain went from the idea of a rewrite to the decision to attempt contacting another friend. Looking back, I think I was too physically exhausted to consider writing a nicer good-bye letter.

Part of the suicide note expressed determination to not "make the same mistakes" I made in January that led to my hospitalization. The chief of these had been to allow anyone to know the extent of my despair. Yet this time, here I was the next day attending IOP, anxiety-ridden and overwhelmed, admitting the weekend's struggle.

I was asked why I think I keep trying to survive. I did not know. I still do not know. Is it God's Spirit? Is there a desire for life somewhere deep inside? Am I just motivated to spare my sons? Whatever the reason, here I am again making efforts to reach out, be loved, and stay alive.

9-1

"Talk about a no-win situation! Sheeeez, you can turn anything into a negative!" Dr. Jay is good-humoredly picking up again on his original intent to rouse some positive self-worth out of me.

"I have thought of depression as something that weaves itself throughout every moment regardless of what you're feeling. Either you are depressed or you are not. So in a good moment, like if one of my sons were to say to me he accomplished something, I could feel really proud, and have the thought 'I shouldn't feel good' at the same time," I say. A doctoral intern asks, "So would that be a good moment or a bad moment?"

"It would be a good moment but I would be denying it. I would be aware I am proud of my son. I would be denying it is good enough to qualify as the opposite of depression. What I need to do is give credence to those moments."

A new woman to IOP interjects. "So you are putting quality on it? 'You're not as depressed as you could be' still sucks."

"I see where you are coming from," I say. "Do you want to eat the apple in the mud or the apple the dog peed on?"

She gets it. "Exactly! And people are saying, 'Great! You have an apple!'"

Moods are a state, they change with how we think about things. Is it cold, hot, rainy, sunny? What people say or do not say, what we are wearing, sitting on, what we have eaten, whether we have eaten, these all affect mood. Moods cannot stay the same. Maybe wanting to feel better seems foreign to me because I think saying I want it would be acknowledging I have been doing wrong all this year. More guilt.

"What if you have made mistakes all year long?" Dr. Jay responds to my expression of these thoughts.

"You feel like you can't make mistakes." The new member directs her comment at me.

"Not in every area of life," I protest. "I mean, if I make a typo, it's okay."

Guffaws fill the room.

"Really?"

"Typos? You suck."

"Oh my, no!"

"I shouldn't have used typos as an example. I'm a writer, they matter!" I laugh.

Dr Jay teases, "I wish I knew that before I let you in this program, Nancy."

"Well, yeah, I'm almost obsessive about typos," I say. "Honestly, I can make mistakes, just not the kind I think shame is attached to."

"Why?"

"Because shame sucks," the woman answers.

"But what if we've already done things we are ashamed of?" Dr. Jay asks.

"I don't know!" The woman comments sarcastically toward our ill-treated group leader. "That's your job. That's why I'm paying you the big co-pays!"

Dr. Jay shakes his head in mock exasperation. "I need to do a better screening job here!"

Laughter is lifting all of our moods at the moment.

I shift directions. "My attitude about getting involved is changing. Now I am asking, 'what if?' Trying to focus on what I want rather than on what I shouldn't be doing."

Finally, Dr. Jay has an opportunity to be pleased. Grinning, he says, "It's rubbing off."

"I decided whatever I do at church is to be a team effort. I can't afford emotionally to be doing life by myself anymore. Leadership positions tend to be Lone Ranger so I want to stay out of that for at least awhile."

A chorus of affirmative responses follow this statement.

"Absolutely!"

"That is so cool, gives me hope."

"Great idea!"

"Then I was very open with Lynne. It is hard for me to expose some information, and I have recently been saying, 'here it is.' I'm sharing secrets I have never talked about," I add.

"Good for you, you are trusting that much." Dr. Jay encourages me.

"It's hard, but it's good."

"Nancy, notice it is good. That it's safe."

At this point in the conversation, I feel it is time to let him in on a truth he may have missed.

Self-consciously I continue. "When I rolled my eyes at you two days ago, and we were joking around about disrespecting you well, I want you to know that rolling my eyes at you is the exact opposite of disrespect. Because I would not allow other people to know I have a problem with that issue. That's hard for me, and I was letting you know."

"Thank you," he says sincerely.

Needing comic relief, I follow up with, "So, I'm going to roll my eyes at you more often."

"Ha,ha, that's great!"

9-2

This past year there has been much wrestling with God over timing. He is with me here now, in this life. In the land of the living. Nonetheless, I keep pushing to be with him in heaven. What has to be number one priority is that I get back to where I fully trust him.

Why am I not taking medications as prescribed? There has been such spiritual confusion and grief over the distance I sense between us. Why the pervasive, continuing self-sabotage? It goes back to the push-pull relationship I am having with God. He is not pushing or pulling, it is I doing that. I have not trusted him.

Keeping these negative behaviors is refusal to make the commitment to put them aside for good. That is what I mean by getting back to where I can leave things in his hands; to be certain suicide is not what he wants for me, and not questioning that. Believing he knows best. Relying on his process.

Finding proof of his trustworthiness is easy. Certainly, there is not one day that could pass I would not see evidence of that fact. When I was a teenager and pursuing negative goals, is when Christ found me. He introduced himself as my good shepherd, and that is when this sheep chose to turn from the edge of a cliff and follow him. I feel rescued.

How can I move forward from past regrets, present sorrows, and suicidal thoughts? I need to do the things I know increase faith like spending time reading the Word of God. However, I am having trouble with that just now. The disease of Major Depression is still hindering my understanding. It is not a problem of opening the book and recognizing passages that apply to me; it is a problem of application. This leads to the next need, to be around Christian women.

The line-up must make everything that is peripheral secondary in order to get back to where I am truly allowing Christ to be the difference maker instead of doing it myself.

9-7

Give up. Try. Give up. Try again. Keep trying. Another round of try.

The *why* of all this effort toward behavior and thought pattern changes eludes me. The reason why I have hung on to the idea of suicide is easier to come by. Suicide seems to offer hope to me. It is because I do not believe my situation, especially my marriage, will get better. I need to trust God's ideas are best, yet I genuinely do not want to go on. That is why I keep playing with it, even trying to get back to the point where I do not care at all, to get past the conviction and do what it is I really want to do.

Lynne tells me it is God's Spirit in me, drawing me to trust and believe God. Ultimately, I want to honor him. Still, it is a war.

"You're playing Russian roulette," she says. "You are getting better; it is not as bad as it used to be. But that does not mean you are out of the woods. I cannot stress enough how foundational this decision is. I'm not hearing you have made a commitment to live."

"No, I have not."

"Why are you shaking?" Lynne asks with concern.

"It's just fear. Sometimes it is more noticeable than at other times."

9-9

Today, journaling just one hour's typical train of thought and behavior, the spin cycle of mood shifts became glaringly clear. No wonder my knees threaten to buckle under me!

1. Need to cheer up. Open the blinds and let light into the apartment.
2. Sad. Do not want the future, so want to stay sad with intention of getting to the point I could end it all. Put on mellow music.
3. Receive a funny note from Tim. Laugh and reply.
4. See on Facebook the names of friends who are gone out of my life. Grieve.
5. Reread some old journaling from this year and see the progress. Feel ashamed for being self-destructive this week.
6. Am reminded through the journaling notes that I made a decision to refocus on life back in May. Feel guilty for not sticking to the daily schedule and for entertaining opposing thoughts.
7. Reread the skills necessary to get out of self-destructive thoughts. Feel empowered to do something about them.
8. Look at the calendar. Am overwhelmed.

9. See the dark future as I have seen it all this year. Sense an overwhelming urgency to end it all.

10. Receive a message from one of my "adopted" young people in Ohio, a twenty-two-year-old man asking me for my prayers and expressing love to me. I reply that I love him too and am praying. I know I cannot hurt him by killing myself. What explanation could anyone give him that would be enough; or give to all the young people who trust me?

11. Reread the reasons I returned to IOP in July. Am surprised to see some progress.

12. Urgency thoughts increase in intensity and number. Must kill myself now before I get beyond the ability to do it!

13. Instead, I write out this thought process to show to Dr. Jay or Lynne to gain some perspective. Also, feel great fear at the idea of sharing this paper with anyone.

14. Sad, but questioning whether I want to be

15. Receive a promising message concerning future prospects. Feel so afraid! Why can't I just end it now?

Steady, Nancy. Hold on!

9-13

Last night's call to the national suicide hotline, 1-800-273-TALK, leads to a return call this morning. A youngish-sounding woman says, "You seem like an intellectual, an analytical person. You have the ambivalence, which is important; you are thinking for the sake of other people reasons why you do not want to commit suicide. But it is something you can have for yourself, too. You need some part of the future to connect to emotionally because logic can go badly. It can reason away those incentives."

Jon called me last night and stayed on the phone for seven hours. Logically, it does not make sense to consider how I feel about missing something in the future because if I am dead I will not care. What about my son? Whom would he have had to call last night if I were not here? I realized as he was talking that he was basing his next decision on my advice. If I had died, what would he have learned?

Talking to the hotline volunteer last night let off steam like the old adage says. The lid on a pot of boiling water will rattle and bang due to the force of the steam pressing against it, until the cook comes along and lifts it. Then the pressure is released and the lid can be still until the buildup repeats.

I have been asked before, "Will you please call me if you plan to hurt yourself?" To which I have always replied, "If I have the wherewithal to call you, I have the wherewithal to not hurt myself." This time I looked at it from a more "gray" perspective and allowed that the phone call could be made *before* I reach the point of no return.

9-20

I called TALK again last night, and the volunteer said I am flirting with suicide but am also flirting with life. It is an interesting perspective. I feel trapped, and sometimes I get angry with Dr. Jay for calling me and making me go to the hospital last January. Then I let him off the hook and get mad at myself for not making my attempt work.

Three days ago, this flirting with suicide impulsively moved into a reckless, dangerous act, with the potential to cause disastrous harm to my body. Depression causes distorted thinking. If in my clearest thinking I can make a solemn covenant to choose life, it would assure those people who seem interested that in moments of my less than clear thinking I will be safe.

Moving regardless of feelings is still a struggle. Smiling by habit, carrying on conversations as if on autopilot and forcing myself to be where these things are expected is wearing me out. I may arrive at an event early, however will wait in the car until late to avoid some awkward small talk. Truth be told, being with people has generally energized me in the past.

This positive effect is lesser at present, and social activities are followed by going to my car and crying. At least I am doing more than a few months ago. Having signed up for teamwork involvements, there are goals I do not want to quit. That is new. Recent changes are stressful in that they are challenging and pushing all the wrong emotional buttons. I feel threatened and overwhelmed. Nonetheless, some healthy buttons are also being pushed, and I have to keep moving.

I whisper again to the wary little girl inside, "Just walk."

Exiting the Tomb

9-27

Ambivalence, refusing to make a quality decision for life while at the same time walking forward, has been prolonging my suffering as Dr. Jay and Lynne said it would. So many times, I have come to the place where I have "chosen" to keep going. It has been similar to having the little devil on one shoulder and an angel on the other, each whispering in my ear. I have allowed myself to be dragged about by whims of emotion, making one healthy decision after another, only to follow the tug of depression once again.

It is time to cut the cord.

I know I have said this before. Motivated by shame and fear of losing or never gaining respect, I have said I would do the right thing. Spurred on by powerful doubt as to whether God would remain pleased with me if I failed to do well, I steered away from suicide. Propelled by an unseen force of guilt, I tried repeatedly to make amends for any poor choice by following through with a healthier choice. All of this, all of it, was regardless of an underlying hopelessness about my future. A persistent sense of dread.

In this limbo, I keep going back to wondering why people want to live. Moreover, should I not want that for myself?

The bottom line is I do not believe my life to be that valuable in the first place. Sure, I can do some good. Perhaps I can be a helpful person, experience some occupational success, maybe even one day Jerry and I will get along famously. Just by staying alive, I know I would prevent some hurt for others. But so what? I am expendable. I do not personally value my life, value living.

Would it really matter if I left? The woman on the crisis line said, "You need to ask yourself what investment you have in the future. What it is you don't want to miss."

There is not anything I will miss about being here if I am dead. I have not been thinking choosing life for my sake is a good enough reason. It is not logical. Since sadness prevails in my heart, how could living be a decision in my best interests? She has me asking a different question. What if my investment in the future was to live my life; to see value in existing; to want to stay around for the whole game just because God gave life to me?

What if my life is worth saving just because I am alive? What if there is value in that?

"Just walk" has brought me this far. So close now to the edge of the tomb's doorway, I can clearly see what is outside, or think I can. Either way, nothing but a willful, deliberate dive back to the slab could prevent my progress.

Lynne has been asking me for months to sign a "Commitment to Living" paper. Signing it would mean accepting once and for all that there is no escape; that when life gets hard, when Major Depression comes, I will choose to manage rather than control the outcome. Signing it means telling God I will trust him for the end story. It means accepting responsibility for taking care of me.

Making this promise to never again attempt suicide means I may be here for my fiftieth anniversary, continue to invest in my sons' lives, and hold grandchildren. It means God will continue to use me for the good of others. Perhaps I will finish a book, sell an artwork, or both. Maybe significant people in my life will value me after all, and just maybe I will learn to love myself.

Like when I punch an old pillow and dust particles fly up and fill the air, is what has been going on in my head. My old, comfortable, familiar beliefs are being smacked. Particles of doubt and countless thoughts are swirling in my head. New vocabulary, new questions, new perspectives.

What if?

What do I want?

It is okay to get my needs met.

It is okay to want to feel good.

These changes have been frightening. Momentarily blinded by the magnitude, the sheer number, and weight of these many considerations, I felt a desperate need to escape. After all, changing one's entire worldview is unsettling at best. I was overwhelmed. Flirting with suicide one last time a few weeks ago, allowed more shame to quickly join the churning cloud in my head and added to the pressure.

"You can't improve your future?" is a challenge broached to me in various forms over the last few months. Possible answers to the question, "What hadn't I tried before?" boiled down to one simple truth. I had never utilized available support and instead had been attempting to live my life on my own. This Lone Ranger existence was failing miserably. It was time to try something new.

What do I need by way of support? Obviously, this requires being where people are. Tentatively, I signed up for church involvements that include teamwork and turned down opportunities that would have isolated me. Joining Dr. Jay's post-IOP Depression Support Group and a Writer's Group are also ways to incorporate this new idea. Opening up to Lynne more completely, taking risks at admitting secrets in group, and just being honest in a couple new friendships are helping to open my path.

Just walk. One day at a time, one meeting at a time, one relationship at a time, one prayer at a time. Allow transformation slowly to take place.

There is a story about a father whose young son was trying hard to move a large rock in their path. The boy tugged and pulled, pushed, and groaned. Placing his back on the rock and planting his feet firmly against a tree, the boy grimaced, straining every muscle to no avail. Quitting, he sank to the ground.

His father asked, "Son, did you use all of your strength?"

"Yeah, dad! I used all my strength."

"Did you try everything you knew to do?"

"Dad, I pushed, I pulled. I tried everything."

"You didn't use all your strength or available knowledge, son. You didn't ask me for help."

Dust is settling today. It is partially because of my choice to stand still. Instead of allowing emotional chaos, I am reaching for one speck of dust at a time, looking it over, and doing what needs to be done with it. Many beliefs and vocabulary words are up for inspection. Negative ones are destined for the trash pile. Well, some will remain. This is going to take awhile.

There seems to be a mixture yet of courage and fear, hopelessness and yearning. I feel I am determined one moment to face life with dignity, maturity, and responsibility. Then the next I am nursing ideas of escape.

There is always the proverbial man with no feet to consider. While I cry about having no shoes, he struggles. Depending on the care of others for his basic needs, he calls out and people come. He is not afraid to admit, "I have no feet" or "I need your help, would you carry me today?" If he is afraid, he is doing it anyway.

What does he have I do not have? Nothing, except a wherewithal to keep on living with hope. So maybe I will wind up always barefoot, hobbling over a stony path and challenged by pain. Still, I can walk. I have been given the tools to build a whole new mindset, a blueprint for a "Can Do" attitude that includes being willing to ask for help.

Now if only I will exit this tomb. Jesus has never quit calling. He has brought people into my life who are offering their hands for support. I am blessed, so very blessed to have them here. I do not have to try to do this on my strength alone.

There is a path to walk. Whether or not I can see around each bend and ascertain why I am going there is moot. Walking is my purpose. The path's existence is enough reason to strive. Allowing others to walk with me is my goal for today.

Finally, by signing the "Commitment to Living Vow," I step out into the daylight.

IT TAKES A VILLAGE TO FREE BOUND HANDS AND FEET

9-28

"This sickness will not end in death," I read aloud.[2] Jesus spoke these words when he learned Lazarus was ill. He did not rush to his dying friend's side to spare him his suffering or impending doom. "This is for my Father's glory," Jesus added, meaning that this sickness would end with people being awed by God.

Lazarus walked out after four days of being buried and an unknown length of time being ill. His feet and hands were still wrapped and Jesus instructed the small crowd to free him. Perhaps my sickness is not supposed to end in death either. Possibly, outside of the tomb there will be people willing to unwrap the linens and help to free me if I give them a chance.

My newly formulated "Safety Plan" is comprised of three phone calls. In the case of self-destructive thoughts I feel are spiraling out of control, I am to reach out to the National Suicide Crisis Line, Lynne, and a third person. At first, it seemed the safety plan might be limited to two calls. Of course, none of this was official anyway, until I told someone of my new commitment. Emailing Dr. Jay, I asked if he would consider being the third emergency connection.

As soon as I pressed SEND, my eye began nervously to twitch. How strange that choosing life would create such anxiety.

Within a few hours, he responded, "In the beginning you will (as you have already) experience fear and doubt. That will fade."

Blind to the truth of this promise, it was all I could do to see hope in the next step, let alone down the road.

10-5

For a full week, my body has reacted to the stress of letting go of my escape plan. The eye twitch finally stopped today.

10-10

Hopping on that round of try, only this time with support in mind, has led to the following changes:

1. Started to take care of my health with the help of others
2. Clued our marriage counselor in on what I am feeling
3. Created and am following my safety plan
4. Joined the depression support group
5. Joined teamwork efforts at church such as a social committee, and by signing on as Bible Study class administrator
6. Upon hearing that people at church are uncertain how to befriend newcomers or support the hurting, and are afraid to do so, I decided I would like to influence in any way I am able how people can better reach out. Five weeks ago I began a Bible Study newsletter, which includes ways to connect more meaningfully with other Bible Study members. I am also slated to teach practical application in Sunday School on the topic of how to be effectively supportive to hurting people without becoming personally overwhelmed.
7. Joined a writer's group.
8. Made a commitment to life and signed the Commitment to Living Vow.

"So, there have been a lot of changes in the last few weeks," I say after reading this list to the small support group that has gathered .

"You are just doing phenomenally!" Dr. Jay says. "What do you think of all you just read?"

"Seeing it all in one place, I guess it looks kind of amazing."

He raises his eyebrows, challenging me to fully accept the good.

"For someone who thought so little of themselves, that's great!" another attendee observes.

"Then as for all this stuff that is going on, there are different feelings mixed in. It doesn't take any effort to feel that heaviness, it is just there. I don't have to dig it up," I say.

"Yes. But I would imagine it is not there as often," Dr. Jay suggests.

"I'm gonna tweak that a little bit- it's there, I think, all the time. But it's less powerful."

"Even better. I guess what I meant is that you are not always mindful of it. You can draw attention to it, and if there is nothing else going on you can think about it."

Group members can relate to this aspect of depression. "Once the negative takes over, it consumes you. It's gonna be there for us. It's a matter of not allowing ourselves to dwell on it. If you are doing something positive, you might be down a little bit- but you can push back," someone says.

"And that would explain then why when there's a pause, deep sadness is there," I add.

"Right," says Dr. Jay.

A woman speaks up. "I listen to Nancy and her problems, and they are horrible to her. I sit back and wonder what do I have to worry about? But depression is still there. I don't care what my problems are, they are horrible to me."

"Exactly." Dr. Jay nods.

The woman continues. "If you can't get rid of it, you have to do something. People don't understand, they think I just need to snap out of it. But there is something up here" —she points to her head—"that is making me feel I am just waiting to die now, and that idea needs to stop."

"Finding things to do is something we talk a lot about in this group. And when we are not busy, we have lots of time to think. Which is typically when it tends to be the negative stuff we conjure up." Dr. Jay turns to me again. "Your mind works like the New York stock exchange ticker board. With depression, there is a 'stock' running across the board every few seconds. We have to fill that ticker with other thoughts and ideas so that the depressive ones can be shoved to the background. That's the challenge. Making the exchange."

In reflection on what supportive persons have been trying to tell me; that my suicide would be a negative, I realize I have not been able to grasp the opposite that my survival could be a positive that would really matter. Maybe this is an exchange worth the work.

10-11

I wake up every morning with dread. My first thought is "I don't want to live another day." It takes awhile to get some energy, and I remember mornings have been like this for decades. Even my old, "Good morning, Lord" was not perky. It was more like, "Oh well, good morning Lord."

Some of that is because of where my focus has landed. It may be a habit by now to expect each day to be lonely and hard despite plenty of evidence to the contrary such as friendships and children. My eyes have remained on Jerry.

I do not think that for most of thirty years he has addressed me using my name unless he was annoyed. He called me Nancy in a normal tone the other day and I was surprised. I have lived my marriage working to satisfy a critical man who seemed to not consider me. Having already lost myself before we became a couple, I wonder if I ever had me. Somehow I handed the reins to decide who I am over to my husband.

He readily admits he has these issues. He will say, maybe even tearfully, how much he loves me and wants to be a better person. I hope he means it enough to take action, because we have had short-lived marital revivals before. I have been trying this year, without much will, to give us yet another shot at trust and happiness. We both need to change. Although we are somewhat pleasant people who are good at being friends in public, our marriage is not a union of two. It is a union of one and his half-person wife.

10-12

Lynne is sympathetic. "Okay. You still have to deal with significant emotional deregulation. You signed the contract, but ever since there have been tremendous emotional problems. The asset is you're very honest when you come in here. And there's movement. But life can throw all kinds of things at you."

"Exactly." Tearfully, I begin to confess the most piercing pain of the past eighteen months, what had so far been too difficult to describe.

"I guess I want to know why God allowed all the circumstances to happen as they did after we came to Pennsylvania. Did he design it? How is it so many details that were out of my control led to such aloneness? Then when I was praying for healing from several illnesses in the spring of last year, was it him telling me to go off medications?"

My breaking heart pleading for an answer, I continue. "Did God orchestrate all this? Did he lead me to attempted suicide, knowing I would survive, so he could ultimately teach me how to live? That's my question."

Lynne looks surprised. "What do you think?"

"When I view the details individually, I can see maybe God had me in isolation for awhile. I am not claiming to understand the reason, but it makes sense he may have had one. It does boil down to that med situation. Other illnesses, including Sciatica, went away after my prayer that day and have not come back. Depression might have also been cured if I had not gone back on meds, right? I think I can see where the rest of these questions fit under the umbrella of 'God knows and I don't have to know.' But the meds thing is just blowing my mind."

I can barely speak. "This confusion has caused me to be afraid to talk with him. What if I misunderstand again? That's been the stake in my heart, Lynne, losing communication with God. It's still raw, and I don't know how to get back.

"I don't mean he cut me off," I say. He is trying to help me somehow. He put up the barriers for a reason, led me down this path for a purpose, and I don't know what those are."

Lynne adds gently, "It sounds like it is very, very hard for you to just let that go. To move on and continue trying to hear the voice of God."

"Think about the year before we moved, Lynne. In the winter of two thousand and nine, there was much negativity going on in our marriage, and I was diagnosed with six different health problems, three of them major and lifelong. I was working two part-time jobs, going to school full-time, and insomnia had me awake two to four nights a week. In all that stress, I had a joy that did not make sense. It came from watching the *Matthew* movie, the dramatized reading of the Bible book. Over the course of several weeks, children at a mission's afterschool care program followed that gospel story with me. We were watching Jesus unfold in front of us. Nothing topped that joy.

"In the spring on the last day of work there before summer break, fully expecting to return in the fall, I believed the Lord told me I wouldn't be coming back. He directed me to start shutting down my second job and to say goodbye to my clients there. It was clear to me life was going to change drastically, and in prayer I prepared. Finally, I knew I would be saying goodbye to my sons."

"That was before you knew about the move?" Lynne asks.

"Yes. Do you see the theme? God was *talking* to me. I *knew* what he was saying to me. When we arrived here, I found myself with free time. Two to three hours a day, I would study the Bible, pray, and memorize scriptures. I asked him, 'What in my life needs to be cleared up?' One thing that came to mind was that in setting my own agenda each day I was trying to control the nuances of my life. Therefore, I started sitting down every morning and asking him what my schedule was for the day, then I would write down my thoughts. It was amazing. No matter how long the list was, each day that I followed it in the order it came to me I was finished by the time Jerry got home. Each time.

"Lynne, do you see now why what happened last year is confusing? In light of the fact God's direction is usually clear to me, and the daily communing with him, I am supposed to second-guess about the medications? That's one of the reasons I struggle to take them as prescribed now. I think maybe Dr. Jay, Kelly, pastors, and friends find it easy to say, 'Oh you misunderstood. That was the depression talking.' But they don't know the context."

"Yes." Lynne is reflecting on what I said. "So, since that time you've not been able to hear God?"

"I'm afraid, so afraid I'll get it wrong. Since the day I went back on meds, we haven't had that time in the morning. I feel like I blew it by taking them again. If that is true, then everything that happened afterward is my fault. The depression, the attempt, all of it. If it was depression, and not God telling me to go off of the medications, then I misunderstood and can no longer know his leading."

Lynne points out a distortion. "Do you recognize the black and white thinking?"

"No."

"If you blew it, then everything...? I have to think most of us trip up on the little things in life, that we are not tuned in to his voice as you are describing. I would think that is rare."

"Maybe I got proud and had to be knocked down a peg," I say.

Lynne disagrees. "In the scriptures, we see Jesus was approachable and patient, and that he is the exact representation of God. I don't have all your answers, but I don't think Jesus was just waiting to slap you back; that the first time you didn't hear his voice perfectly he dropped the bottom out of your life."

"I don't look back on this year and in any way feel like God let me down. Not at all. I just question if he designed it all for a reason."

Lynne pauses and speaks carefully. "It gets murky. I can see this is such a pivotal and big thing for you. Nancy, Sciatica is a specific problem. Depression has many components. You have had trauma you have not made sense of, a difficult marriage you are living in, the cognitive work you've been doing... this is what I am thinking. God gives us insight to who he is so we can accept salvation. After that, it is a process. Growth comes by learning over time. There is no 'zap' followed by all our distorted thinking having been replaced with truth and good thinking."

Several minutes of silence follow as I ponder this.

"You're right, that makes sense." Another long pause as a memory surfaces in my mind.

"Lynne, you are making me remember something I could apply here. When I was about nine or ten years old, a dentist slapped me across the face because I complained I could still feel the pain when he started to pull a tooth. He told me to stop crying, I said that it's still not numb, then he smacked me. Hard. I had a fear of dentists for a long time. So much fear, that at twenty-five years of age, I had a four year-old abscessed tooth. I absolutely refused to do anything about it for four years. I would eat on the left side of my mouth for *four years*. It got so bad it was actually growing out of my jaw, and I couldn't close my teeth."

"Oh, Nancy!" Lynne is startled.

"I spent a year trying not to close my mouth completely. It was insane. Of course I realized it was insane and becoming more so. All the while, I was feverishly praying, 'Jesus, please heal my tooth. Please.' Nevertheless, I had to go through with getting dental help. I learned this dentist was not abusive; it was safe after all. If God had just healed me at that time there would have been other issues, like a lifetime fear of dentists, for instance."

Now I am thinking aloud. "Just never applied that lesson to this situation. I don't understand why I heard that I was supposed to go off meds, especially since that was asked specifically. It does make sense God would not have just wiped away depression. If he had, I would not have the incentive to look at how I deal with people or to know about black and white thinking. Jerry and I would not be in marriage counseling. If you look down the whole string of changes made this year... I would not be in counseling or involved in any support groups, but would still be floundering around by myself. It makes a lot of sense, Lynne. I don't have to know the why. I don't have to know what exactly transpired that day."

"Nancy," Lynne comforts me. "There are things we won't know until we see him face to face. And then I have the feeling it won't matter."

"You're right. It won't."

10-14

Talking matters out is healing. Discussing them with a knowledgeable and sensitive person makes all the difference in the world. As Lynne figuratively labored at unwrapping my hands, the thought came to me that God did hear my prayers concerning depression and is continuing to do so. He is choosing a means different than my black and white interpretation would allow. Remembering what my prayers had been: teach me, help me grow, deal with my sins; it looks as if he had it all under control from the beginning.

For instance, in the months when a desperate, crushing pressure nearly controlled each minute, I had IOP, and group members there. Maybe receiving that initial basic teaching allowed my mind to be open to different interpretations of the past when the unloading of it finally began. When I lost hope in finding that individual counselor, a credit card issue led me eventually to Lynne. In the meantime, Rose appeared on the scene and gave me an outlet. Which will I focus on? Plenty of pain and confusion could hold the spotlight. Nonetheless, God is good all the time, no matter how I feel.

Maybe that is why faith is not a matter of sight. I can be so blind.

10-23

Paying attention to my feelings means keeping track of where they are on life's roller coaster. This weekend's thoughts? *I don't know why I am still here. Nothing, not one aspect of life seems worth it. I signed the Commitment form, knowing full well I meant to keep those promises. Now I care very little if I keep those promises or not. I know that is wrong. But I don't care.*

When this type of mood increases in strength, it is time to take inventory of any red flags of depression that are waving. What is happening?

Isolating:	not calling friends back; cancelling plans
Negativity:	focusing more on negative thoughts; negative belief system is activated

Activity level:	less interested in hobbies; staying in bed; frittering time away
Situation (stressors):	grief; reminiscing with a relative; regrets
Ask:	how long have these red flags been waving? (One week) How intensely do I feel these on that 10-1 downward scale? (3)

Now is the time I must interrupt this thought cycle.

Management of emotions is possible. The difficulty lies in wanting to. Depression saps motivation. This is why having the Mental Health Wall is important. Without much effort, I can read solutions offered by supports. My plan of action to interrupt the backslide is to keep moving regardless of how I feel, to remember the cons to letting myself slide, to challenge the evidence of negative beliefs, and to work.

This morning we went to church. I was tearful the whole time. Exhausted, I could not fathom going to Sunday School and facing people. Instead, I went home while Jerry finished his sound tech duties in the services. It was the right choice. While fighting depression with an action plan makes sense, one must also bear in mind the continuum. Not taking on too much is strategic as well. Putzing for two hours, the apartment was cleaned and some other light work was accomplished.

Feeling so much better, I could participate in a little marriage counseling homework, a conversation that unlocked difficult subjects. Namely, Jerry feels unloved and disrespected, and I feel as if I have lost myself. The conversation is not over, but the door has been flung wide open.

10-25

Mikey was the puppy that replaced Andy in our home. He was a Rottweiler, German Shepherd mix. He was with us for two years when suddenly, due to circumstances out of our control, we found ourselves at the veterinarian's office asking for Mikey to be put down.

This decision had not been difficult to make because the situation sadly called for it. In typical fashion, my feelings were left out of the picture. Since the choice was obvious, what business was it of mine to feel anything, right?

I have been pretty much out of touch with my emotions all my life. When they are overwhelming is when all the years of practice shoving them back down kicks in the most. Often, I do not know why they come, what they are, or whether I should express them.

It should be no surprise to me then that I stood over Mikey's dying body and fought back the sadness. This was simple. A procedure. There had been no choice.

Wal-Mart was the next errand on the day's list. Inside the store, I thought it odd I was so tired. Still, we completed the shopping and headed out to our car.

My knees buckled. Thankfully, I had the cart to hold me up. Completely unaware of what was happening, I questioned why my hands were shaking, and why I felt faint. Jerry, observing most of this, made one comment that opened my mind for the first time to just how closed my heart could be. "You care more about Mikey than you think you do."

That was twenty-two years ago. Last week, an unexpected phone call came. "Hi, Nancy?" It was an unfamiliar southern voice.

"Yes?"

"This is Janet from Tennessee." That name was not familiar to me.

"I just read your article about depression online. I've read it over and over again. I am wondering if you can help me," she said with a drawl.

"Oh!" Surprised is not a strong enough term for what I felt."I can try."

"I am sure God has left me. I just know I have sinned too much and he has decided he is through with me."

Uncertain what I could do for her, I just prayed. She continued to explain her battle with depression and how recently she had spoken some words she believed were offensive to God. Her pastor and church friends did not understand, and she felt she had nowhere else to turn. One fact was certain; her depression was severe. In the course of her struggle with this disease, she had lost her usual sense of spirituality. No longer could she feel God's presence, or understand his promises as they applied to her. Depression can do that—make a believer feel spiritually dead.

Clarifying to her my lack of professional or educational expertise, I assured her of what I know to be true; God does not walk away when we hurt. The article to which she referred is titled, *Never Alone in the Dark: A Christian's Experience with Depression.* In it, I describe my own struggle with spiritual life during one major depressive episode endured a few years ago. It mentions that although a sense of God's comfort was missing during the ordeal, and all vestiges of religion were gone, he had not stood back and waited for my confused mind to become reasonable. The last words read, "It is a rather simple bottom line—when all else was lost, Christ was there. And he never let me go."

Hopefully, Janet was encouraged by our phone conversation. We were on dangerous ground because she was asking for a diagnosis in some ways. All I could safely offer was my personal experience and a few scriptures. After she agreed to find both a psychiatrist and therapist, we said goodbye.

Spurred on by the pain in Janet's voice, and in recalling my own unexpressed anguish over the years, courage to tell what I know has grown. Other experiences as a church leader, such as being told to keep my dirty laundry at home, and listening to prayer requests week after week that never express anything personal, joined with the sad fact of having once been a judgmental silencer myself, show I have something of a unique point of view to offer. Namely, that Christian churches are full of hurting believers who are quietly withholding their doubts and questions, and walking through life in isolation.

Some of us have been abused; some have been the abusers. Trauma of various sorts has numbed even the most sensitive of hearts among us, and lousy coping mechanisms have destroyed families, and peace. Two things have to change; people like me have be open to feelings and to the humility of expressing them, and the Church has to learn that emotionally struggling people are in the pews and that this is *normal*. Christians like Janet and I need to be spared condemning remarks and judgmental attitudes. Otherwise, how can any of us get well?

The challenge for both the church-at-large and me is the same. Be real.

10-30

Still wavering in mood.

The three reasons it is good to be alive have not yet come to me. There is no comparison to being with Christ in eternity, and I want to be with him in heaven and be at peace. Maybe I am just being stubborn. Around me is a world of suffering—people in pain who have not quit and do not want to quit. Why they are hanging on is a mystery to me. It is not a familiar concept, loving life.

Dr. Jay's email, sent after I signed the vow, included a statement suggesting strength in my confidence to live could grow. That too, has been elusive. In the last month, my safety plan has been activated four times. Making those contacts brought on the usual sense of foolishness and shame, and my powerful draw to suicidal thoughts was compounded. Yet only briefly.

Confidence to live has peeked over my walls just a bit, however. I had been avoiding the topics of mental illness and depression in my preparations for teaching the Sunday School class, in order to prevent self-exposure. Now I see that is the only way to go. In coming to that conclusion, and in thinking of creative ways to get my points across, my confidence does grow.

11-2

Marriage counseling has opened a line of communication between Jerry and I that most likely would have remained closed. Doug has been challenging us to look deeper into exactly how we are each affecting the other's sense of well-being through our behavior and words. As a result, Jerry has agreed to his own individual counseling. I watch as he goes through doubts and resistance similar to what I first experienced. For people who think in black and white terms, waiting on a slow process that has more gray than Cleveland skies is frustrating. In time, he will catch on.

11-6

Those promises from Dr. Jay have been a lifeline over the past six weeks.

"As you gain strength in your confidence to *live* don't be surprised by the grace that the Lord begins to bless you with! In the beginning you will (as you have already) experience fear and doubt. That will fade."

For me, the "grace" God is blessing me with, which is indeed surprising me despite being warned not to let it, is showing up in a growing attitude of "this may not be so bad after all." Our pastor preached on the word "Go" from the challenge Jesus left with his followers, and my heart was stirred again to the idea of making a significant difference in this world. The future still looks bleak and scary—health, personal value, and love remain in question. Yet there is strength in my confidence to live that coincides with Dr. Jay's prediction. Fear and doubt about facing life seem actually to be fading. Even though they still can come on with a vengeance, their visits are briefer. Interesting, that I now see their appearances as visits rather than as all of truth for all time to come.

It is similar to going on a trip. People who have been at the destination can describe where travelers are going, and what they will find when they arrive. However, until the novices experience it for themselves there is no way to grasp what or how it will be for them. Being told that God would grant me grace, that fear and doubt will fade, and being encouraged to enjoy life as my confidence to live grows, is to give me an itinerary for a trip I have not yet taken. I can believe my experience will follow that course because a knowledgeable person told me so. However, it is impossible to see, to taste, and to comprehend until it becomes my personal journey.

11-14

The Depression Support Group was not in session when I arrived late tonight. Dumb traffic. I think, *Dr. Jay didn't want to be in a group at all, didn't want to be in a group with me, and left as soon as possible realizing he had an excuse to get out early. Maybe he even moved the group to another venue and neglected to let me know on purpose. Or he is at least glad he forgot!*

Wow, negative belief systems can be insanely unreasonable. If it did not hurt so much, this mindset would be hilarious!

11-21

Thirty years. Jerry and I were married at the ripe old age of twenty. Each of us believed we had a handle on life, and on relating to the other. Soon it became apparent marriage was going to be more challenging than we thought! One great picture of this is the rainy Sunday morning we returned home from church, a few months after our wedding. Standing in the downpour, we searched pockets and my purse for keys. We were locked out. In a matter of seconds, our conversation changed to Jerry blaming me, and me yelling back in defensiveness.

Trying to jiggle windows on the first floor only served to prove their locks worked, and we turned to the basement. On the side of the house was a loose frame surrounding our only hope for entrance. Jerry tugged and pulled; we were soaked, cold, angry, and still sniping about who failed to bring the house keys.

The window was as stubborn as we were. Then Jerry had an idea, which in all fairness, I agreed to. Moments later, he was pushing the window frame out from inside the basement.

The feeling of idiocy in that moment still finds me when I remember that day. In blind anger and pride, we had each lost our senses. Having entered through the unlocked back door, he looked out at me as I stood in the rain, I looked back at him in the light of the basement, and we realized the truth!

I wish I could say we laughed. I wish I could, but cannot. Truth is we stopped talking to each other for a little while. It took a few months to find the humor in that ridiculous moment. However, now it is thirty years later, and the story is funny.

Jerry is learning about distorted thinking in his therapy now too. Yesterday, he said to me, "It's no wonder our marriage has had so many difficult years. We brought loads of false ideas with us." Then choking up a little, he added, "I'm glad we're still together."

Me too.

11-28

About fourteen years ago, a preacher was speaking at a dinner I was attending. Suddenly, in the middle of her speech she stopped, looked over to me, and walked to my seat. Stunned, the crowd and I wondered what this could be about.

She addressed me using a verse from the Bible book of Ezekiel, "He will give you a new heart and put a new spirit in you; he will remove from you your heart of stone and give you a heart of flesh."[3]

It has not been and will not be a quick work.

The experience of Dr. Jay not being in his office when I arrived two weeks ago has been good for me. Therapy and support groups are a type of microcosm of the real world. Learning to deal with reality in the confines of an office and practicing new ways of relating with people who can understand, makes walking among the land of the living more promising.

He explained in an email the misunderstanding. No one had made it and after waiting nearly half an hour, he left. Traffic had caused me to miss him by only five minutes. The bottom line is, he and Lynne, along with my friends, and husband are human and will disappoint me. I will frustrate them, too. If the foundation of these relationships is trust, we will be okay.

On the way to the group session today, the idea occurred to me I could bank this experience. This is that microcosm, right? Relational snags in the future could be dealt with through a withdrawal of this memory, that despite my fears no one rejected me. Then laughing aloud, I thought, *I could deposit this in my "trust fund!"*

Shedding distrust is like Jerry's and my riddance of supposed treasures during our move. Downsizing meant to us selling and giving away almost everything. Like negative beliefs, those material items were serving no purpose, weighing us down, creating chaos, and hard to carry.

We arrived in Pennsylvania with six pieces of furniture, few outfits and shoes, and a roomful of items left to sell that took over a year to purge. Our commitment to more simple living has kept our apartment comfortable.

Eradicating distrust and refusing to replace it with more negativity is a good idea too.

Recurrent Major Depression may come round again someday. Actually, it is likely. If it does, the venomous self-talk may increase in volume, previously challenged negative beliefs may be triggered, and each morning will begin with dread. God will seem incommunicado. Life's value may be held up once again for question; such is the nature of the disease.

11-29

Last weekend, on a trip to the Pocono Mountains, I walked out onto a store's back porch. Surrounded by antique chairs, tables, and benches, an ancient trunk caught my eye. Oblivious to any danger, I turned to get closer to the potential treasure.

Wham! One second I was standing, the next my body was painfully twisted and halfway to the ground beneath the porch. Rotted boards had given way. The floor had literally gone out from under my feet, leaving me beat-up, bruised, and sore since.

Distrust is like that, sometimes fueled by the mood disorder. It is tough to explain; precise words seem evasive. Growth, forward thinking, and even trust are present and then suddenly are not. Something triggers ingrained doubt and it becomes reality obscuring all else, both feelings and facts.

Why is progress in relationships and emotional health so swiftly discarded and replaced by fear? How does it happen that the brain sees clearly what is real yet the heart does not believe? Is meaningful expression of this phenomenon possible?

One can see how that kind of caution is destructive. The grownup conditioned to doubt as a child may manage quite well while relationships are running smoothly. Unchallenged, trust can seem simple.

Then, bam! Out of nowhere, a perceived threat. A chain reaction is set off. First, there is the shock at being knocked out of peaceful reverie, then shame at having foolishly relaxed joins fear of hurt, and before much time passes (maybe immediately), old survival instincts have replaced existing logic.

I imagine this is comparable to the experience of a man who has no interest in daring exploits and yet receives a gift certificate for a free bungee jumping course. He feels some obligation to the giver and does not want to disappoint. Consequently, the wary recruit slowly makes his way to the site while the question to undertake the exercise or not lingers unresolved in his mind. Each tentative step is agonizing. His natural inclination is to run away, however his original motive and a desire to deny his fear compels him forward. Conversations with regular jumpers and trained professionals draw assurances it is safe.

They show off the equipment as the unlikely participant handles it, tugging, and feeling its strength. It seems it might be secure. He watches as others jump successfully and listens attentively to the experts who seem to know their sport. Only now, it is his turn. Strapped tightly to the bungee cord, he daringly allows his feet to leave solid ground. That is when it hits him.

He is now in mid-air, his fate completely dependent on the honesty and knowledge of the people above.

He might cuss under his breath at this point or scream loudly. He possibly thinks, *This cord might break, or they may walk away and leave me dangling here, and it will be my fault for trusting.*

Allowing built-in fears to override current reality is similar to that scenario, except the one conditioned to doubt experiences the walk to the bungee jump site each time they have an opportunity to trust. Past poor judgment calls have left them sore and more apprehensive than ever. Not only do they struggle to have faith in other people, the terror of having confidence in oneself is the shaky base underneath it all.

Testing the floorboards in relationships while hoping for the best yet expecting the worst can dissolve facts into a background of negative beliefs that seem truer.

11-30

There is a culture of the lonely in this world. In America. Only it is not a sub-culture, it is the collective. In homes, offices, schools, and churches people are looking at each other from across the room and not seeing. We are stumbling over each other's steel-gray cages that confine us to our individual thoughts and worries. Where is that open hand of fellowship? It is squeezing the keys tightly in its palm.

The villagers involved in freeing my bound hands and feet are doing double service. As I am liberated, my hands can help to unbind someone else. Then that person can turn and loosen another set of hands, and on it goes. We just have to be willing to be released, and then willing to help release others.

To want a relationship is to be a spot-on image of the Creator. He made us for fellowship with him, did he not? He made us for each other too. He meets our needs through his people, all of whom will fail at their job more than once. Then he holds us, renews our strength in his perfect love, and sends us out to try again with those squirrely creatures called humans. No wonder we hurt. No wonder it seems better to remain emotional shut-ins.

No wonder he promised never to leave us. He knew how desperately we would need to cling to those words.

The End is Never the End

12-1

Paul was an author. A successful one. Thousands heard what he wrote when he was alive, and millions have read his works since his death. There is no question his life held purpose as his pen served to change despair to hope for so many. Moreover, he knew it.

Yet he wanted to die.

Some may argue with me that by suggesting Saint Paul of the New Testament would have preferred death to life I am undermining his true heart. However, in reading his words a familiarity wraps around me. In reflection of Paul's mutually opposed desires, my true heart also wants desperately to be with God. Yet I care deeply about making a positive difference in this world.

Paul was in prison when he wrote the following:

> For to me, to live is Christ and to die is gain. If I am to go on living in the body, this will mean fruitful labor for me. Yet what shall I choose? I do not know! I am torn between the two: I desire to depart and be with Christ, *which is better by far*; but it is more necessary for you that I remain in the body. Convinced of this, I know that I will remain...[4]

While these sentiments were being recorded, Paul's body was probably racked with pain. Numerous beatings, whippings, and imprisonments as well as having been pummeled with rocks until he was nearly dead had no doubt left him with great discomfort. Maybe he was disabled in some way, we do not know. He knew he was likely to face more of the same torture. Many of his closest friends did not live nearby and there was no phone or internet by which to receive encouragement. He was aware he might never visit with some of them again. People he should have been able to trust were backbiting him and his ministry, even attempting to bring him more trouble. He knew they would likely continue.

Pain, fear, loneliness, betrayal by significant others, his future looked bleak. It does not take much effort at all for me wholeheartedly to believe he would rather have been dead. Nevertheless, his passions included the people to whom he ministered. He chose to continue his work because he felt it was all *worth it*.

Worth it. Who gets to decide the value of a person's struggle?

My contemplative son Tim recently told me, "There is no price too high to pay for a chance to help someone change." He was referring to growing old and becoming physically and perhaps mentally limited. "You may not know what it is," he continued, "but God may use one little thing you say or do to bring about positive change in someone's life. As long as any one of us is breathing, God has a purpose for us here. And it's worth it."

Paul strained against something he figuratively called "a thorn in the flesh." Actual thorns dig under the skin causing it to swell and mercilessly itch. Anyone would want one removed. Who would have thought the persistence of Paul's "thorn" would become a powerful teaching on the grace of God through hard times? Can my own thorn also be a blessing?

It may be, maybe not too, that each day of my future will be a struggle. Right now, tears rise to the surface three or four times daily. Each public appearance, no matter how insignificant, costs me emotionally. Ninety percent of the time, I would rather be dead. If this is my foreseeable future, I still have a reason for staying alive.

Because to be in this world is to live for Christ. He has a purpose for me outside the tomb.

12-15

"Feeling good is better! I know what this feels like and want you to have it." These sentiments worded in a variety of ways are urgently repeated in Dr. Jay's office. I do not know what he is describing, however if I could choose one feeling out of all of life to experience and hold onto, it would be peace.

"Who, me?" Turning to see whom Jesus was inviting to come closer, I realized he was beckoning to me. Surrounded by a mass of people spreading over green hills and mountains, he sat on table rock, holding children on his lap.

In real life, I was twenty-four years old. Nevertheless, in this dream I was five. It was nearly impossible to comprehend he would choose me out of this crowd. Hesitantly I walked toward him, uncertain he would not change his mind.

His eyes were welcoming, piercing straight into my hurting heart. Crawling up on his lap, suddenly I was able to understand that he was holding every individual assembled there simultaneously, loving each equally with all his being.

Sounds like a peaceful wonder on which to focus.

Fearful desperation has overshadowed my lifetime. Once I tried to describe this overwhelming sense to a pastor. "I feel like I am standing in the middle of the road, a semi-truck barreling down on me, and my only escape is to jump aside. Lining the side of the road are myriad snarling dogs, hungrily watching my every move. God is above, waiting to see what choice I will make."

"Nancy, where you are wrong is that God has jumped in front of that truck with you and is going to carry you to safety," he said with intensity.

Two weeks before I tried to end my life, I called for the following toast:

"Let's raise our glasses...here's to a glimmer of hope in the rising of a new dawn, to the next tentative step on a slippery dew-sprinkled path, and to the tenderly firm grip from above by which we are steadied. May this next year be better than the last. Happy New Year!"

It may appear that grip from above failed; that God forgot to rescue me from the truck. However, if allowed to continue the way I had been, nothing at all would have changed. Yes, he let me slip, but he never let go. Through this experience, he is readying me for what may yet come.

1-1

Let's raise our (eye) glasses... May the clarity of hindsight be our catalyst for change, our present focus an exercise in hope, and our visions for the future unveil opportunities to live out faith. May next year be better than the last. Happy New Year!

Each time my life has been derailed by Major Depression renewal has included significant lifestyle changes. Getting married; leaving the workforce to be a stay-at-home mom; and going back to school and finishing my degree are products of recoveries. Although this episode's symptoms were the most severe, the result is similar in that a new career has been launched.

Writing is a way, hopefully an effective one, of battling the stigma of mental illness in the church through education, and offering hope to others who suffer. Based on the many stories people have shared with me and my own experience, I've come to the conclusion Christians in America as a whole need to step up their game in the 'love your neighbor' department. Too many of us go unaided, unaccompanied through life's battles because potential helpers are afraid to get involved. My goal is to invite people to look a little deeper into possibilities. That requires facing my greatest fear— openness and vulnerability.

It is significant to me that I was assigned January 15, 2012, as one of the teaching dates. On the one-year anniversary of the day I decided the pain of living was not worth any good I could accomplish or experience, about fifty people will be hearing ideas on how to better connect with each other and the hurting among them.

One year. A year I did not want to see, a year of change. For me, many of the situations existent twelve months ago remain. Concerns regarding the future are intact. However, now there are potential friendships, black and white thinking and false negative beliefs are being challenged, and I am learning skills for coping no one has taught me before. Most importantly, I am not trying to do life on my own.

Old-familiar threatens to overtake this growth. It is still so very easy to hide in a crowd. I envy open people, admire their courage, and wish I could emulate them. Only one cure for that envy exists. Just talk. Not one for New Year's Resolutions, this time the challenge is obvious. What have I tried before that has not worked? Hiding. What have I not tried that might work? Openness. What kind of person am I? The kind who remains guarded and never gets too close to anyone. What kind of person would I rather be? Honest. Real.

1-6

Jerry and I had our first fight today! Ha-ha. Not really, but it was a rare one that was fought fairly. Our mode of operation in the past has been to accuse and retreat. These "fights" I blamed on his not talking, and he blamed on me for talking too much. It probably did not matter since the result was always the same, two angry and lonely people sitting in the same room in silence.

Not so today! The prizefighter and the underdog met in the ring, both scowling and ready to defend their standing. I have to admit I am the one an audience would bet on because I am quicker on my feet. However, this competitor has a right hook that can send me reeling.

Our referee was in the ring with us. Well, in spirit. What we are learning from our instructors was in our heads. The question was would we play by the rules?

We squared off. The first punch was surprisingly not the last. No one retreated! The prizefighter was stunned and the underdog returned with a blow to the gut.

Okay, now I am just getting silly. No one was actually punching. The words we exchanged were not devastating or accusatory. Oh yes, we were angry. However, what was missing was defensiveness, and silence.

Before too long I realized what I fear was not going to happen. He was not going to walk out of this conversation. He was pleased to find his fear was also not met as his opinions were respected.

This fight actually ended in a resolution. We both won.

1-9

"You do know. You know better." Dr. Jay is challenging my stubborn belief in ancient lies. He has called into question the legitimacy of a voice that has been untruthful for so long.

He is right. I do know. I know to compare evidence for the negative against the opposite.

Other people, men and women who apologize for every move they make, call themselves losers aloud—those are the people with self-esteem issues. Not me, right? I am actively participating in life, not publicly complaining. However, in my head, thoughts go something like, *You stupid idiot. There you go again. Why are you so dumb as to fall for that old trick every time? Believing for a few minutes that you deserve to enjoy that moment, that compliment, that friendship...they all wish you would leave. All the broken relationships that have hurt you are your doing. Your life is meaningless. You will never be free, you deserve what you get. This is payback.*

"I can be so hard on myself."

"I know." Dr. Jay asks with hope, "Can this upcoming weekend be a celebration?"

"Maybe. The voice is just so loud."

1-10

Early this afternoon, I sat in my office chair to begin writing. On the monitor was a remarkable invitation from Jerry.

JOIN IN A CELEBRATION OF THE LIFE OF NANCY Sunday, January 15 Lunch at Bertuccis:
A commitment to life, not only her own but the life of others

- Activist and counselor for pro-life
- Care for the emotionally hurting
- Homeless ministry
- Kids of the inner city

A commitment to Christ

- Ministry to children: Community Program, children's church, Royal Rangers, home school group, annual family events for the community

- Ministry to adults: friend, teacher, singer, newsletter writer, outreach event planner

- Disciple: learning new ways of thinking, new core beliefs, tearing down old ways of thinking, re-evaluating her theology/doctrine

A commitment to motherhood

- Raised two boys

- Home school

- Broke the family chain of destruction

A commitment to Jerry

- Friend: listener, confidant, advice

- Helper: partner, companionship

- Marriage for life

Her own woman

- Business startup

- Writer and author of articles, blogs and books to help people

The "Mental Health Wall" tells the tale...

Love, Jerry

"Pretty awesome what Jerry did, don't you think?" I am asking this of the few people in the know of our situation.

Responses are enthusiastic and confirming.

"WOW! He is getting it."

"Pretty cool, indeed! What a sensitive, compassionate, and encouraging thing to do for you!"

"That's a very nice thing he did!"

1-11

With celebration in mind, Lynne and I intentionally discuss what has deeply changed in my situation and in me, and why living another year has been a positive. Two of the biggest changes are ones in which I still hesitate to put much hope. We are in marriage counseling, and Jerry is in individual therapy.

When I said in the hospital that marriage counseling had to occur in order for me to have any hope, I was actually saying Jerry needs to be fixed. Light has shone on my own blemishes this year, and now I am as equally certain of my need for marriage counseling as I am of his.

Jerry's Major Depression has been the impetus behind much of what he has said to me in the past. His comment about not loving me for ten years? He had explained at the time he was referring to his lack of any feelings at all in any area of his life. My Major Depression would not allow me to hear that last part. I just knew the love of my life hated me.

Oh yes, I recognize the black and white thinking in that statement. Now I do, anyway. Neither one of us can lean back and blame this disease for all our behaviors. There have been choices. It is fair to admit we are two broken people who have mistreated each other in different ways. If I can see that and get better, then I can start to trust he will too.

1-15

I have looked at this day as a threat, primarily because the idea of celebrating survival is half-hearted. No active pursuit of suicide, no plotting, or entertaining suicidal thoughts is happening anymore. That does not mean the thoughts are not there.

Jerry is excited for our special celebration. My feelings are more subdued. There has been interference against my best intentions to focus on the positive this week. Preparations for teaching today my second class on how to help hurting people, was interrupted by a broken printer and physical handicap. Thursday I woke up barely able to move. After a painful few hours, I listened as my doctor handed down another diagnosis—disk disease of the neck. This comes with a guarantee of more flare-ups like the one this week that has taken four days to mend so far.

Despite Jerry's best efforts as creating a pleasant afternoon, I'm distracted. Depression has been trying to sink its teeth deeper into me for days. This is the real pain-in-the-neck.

1-17

It is the one-year anniversary of the night I realized my attempt at dying had failed. It is easy to recall being in the emergency room and angrily fighting against the kindness of strangers. I did not want to be there. I had never wanted to be anywhere less.

Today those old thoughts are growing darker. For twelve months, the desire to live has been hard to pin down; the future remains bleak in important respects.

All the training that has been given to me for denying negative thoughts their power is going to be put to rest today. I am not in the mood for tug-of-war; too much energy has been poured into apprehension of these three days. It may be two o'clock in the afternoon, but with no motivation to do otherwise, I am going to dress in all black and go to sleep. Such is my grief.

1-18

Strange sensation. Obscure thought. Uncertain ground. This morning I woke up feeling that last year is past and now I can go forward. Weird!

1-20

The battle for the mind continues as the inner voice steals my joy. *You don't deserve those kudos. You did everything wrong. They do not really know you. If they did, they would be leaving. People are just being polite, and they will be glad when you are gone.*

Lynne asks, "Whose voice does that sound like?"

"Mine."

"I would think that would make you never want to do anything good."

"I taught, directed, and wrote the curriculum for a children's community program for eight years. After each evening, I would come home and shred myself. Everything was wrong with all I had done." I sighed. "Never mind that attendance grew, and children were responding. My sons and I would often go for a joy ride drive afterward as I was trying to survive emotionally. Because if I went home I would have nothing but that voice."

"Do you argue with that voice?'

"Sure."

She presses, "What happens?"

"I lose."

"Nancy, it sounds really exhausting."

"Yes. It is. Then there is the guilt also, that I am responsible for what negative is going on around me. If I didn't cause it somehow, I'm failing to fix it."

Lynne continues, "There has got to be some way that you can challenge those thoughts...to discover how this deeply entrenched belief came to be, that you are worthless."

1-22

One lifelong struggle has been like ascending a ladder with no top rung. I climb and climb.

This must be the last part. This must be what ends all the effort, I think. Only it is not. Looking above, I see the ladder fades into the clouds. Mounting step after step until exhausted, certainty grows. *Surely I have come far enough, risen high enough. So much time has passed, I must be able to finish.* Only that is not true. The next strain of muscles, every last ounce of courage, lifts me enough to see I am yet at the bottom looking up toward an unachievable, invisible top rung.

Last time I saw Dr. Jay, he asked me if I wanted him to value me because I am depressed and do not value myself, or rather for something he might find valuable to him, something worthy. I voted for the second one. In that brief interchange, I was forced to make a decision. What I saw for the first time is that it might be okay for me to be valued. That it might be *okay. Allowed.* Maybe believing in my value is something I could *choose.*

What is it I have been trying to reach at the top of that ladder? The silent scream is formulating a recognizable thought now. My cry has been for someone, anyone to fill the emptiness inside me. Words fell on unhearing ears because they were impossible to decipher. How could I articulate, "*Make* me valuable?" Of course the resolution did not come. No person can bestow value on another.

Since early childhood the little girl inside has searched to fill a longing. Believing she needed attention, that is all she asked for. Until she is convinced the inner shrieking of *You're worthless, That wasn't good enough, You can't be loved*, are lies, she will continue to climb that ladder and never be at peace.

Jerry's approval has been my ultimate hope. When he fails to make me okay, I am no longer a person in my own right. Doug said I have made Jerry into an idol. Rejection by him (perceived or real) has been fuel for my despair. It is still the fear of future dismissal by him that makes me want to avoid growing any older. Last summer, I said my marriage might not ever get better, and I was asked, "So you should end your life?" I am sure that was meant as a rhetorical question, but I did not hear that. The answer I would have given is "Yes." His esteem is nearly everything to me.

Power to decide my worth was surrendered to hundreds of people throughout my life. Understanding this is freeing. Identifying the genuine need gives me opportunity to figure out how to get it met. Long lapses between affirmations and validation from others, are circumstances that can be less threatening. Their power is dimmed because they are no longer viewed as the antitheses to the solution. Wow. All my life I did not see this.

I believe these revelations can be built upon with the guidance of those collaborating with me. It will be the happiest day of my life when I do not want, need, or strive for value or "proof" I am worth anything, when I do not wake up wondering who is going to care about me today. It will be beyond fantastic to have my own vicious inner voice silenced, and to catch a break from self-hatred and guilt for once.

1-25

Discovery is surprising. Ask an archaeologist, an explorer, or detective. Perhaps years of searching preceded the moment of unearthing that treasure, peering into that cavern, cracking that code. In the same way, a lifetime may seem to have faded away before comprehension flashes in one brilliant epiphany.

Worship usually makes me cry. Songs remind me of God's mercy, and my eyes flood in grateful tears. My understanding of his love has been twisted, however. Mercy has been welcome, not just because I am a member of the fallen human race in need of forgiveness, but because of my belief I am not worth loving and God has been patient and kind to me anyway. Full of pity.

I am discovering his love for me is because I exist, in a similar but perfect fashion to my love for my sons. From the very moment they were presented to me, I saw beauty. No matter what they looked like, smelled like, how they talked to me or acted, I saw loveliness. Even if it was not on the surface, I knew it was in there and could come out with proper nurturing.

It is similar to a plant. No one sees the flower while looking at the seed. The gardener knows there is splendor inside and that it takes patient caretaking for that vision to become reality. In looking at babies, we do not always see the loveliness they will be when they are men or women. We do know it is in there.

That is how I think God sees me. He chose to create and pledged to love me. He actually likes this daughter, and looking past my flub-ups sees all he intended me to become. He is not disappointed or angry that spiritual perfection has eluded me. He knows what the disease of depression is, knows my frailties, and sees beauty. Why did I not understand this before? Did I forget?

There is a fine line between knowing something is true and being able to apply it, and temporarily feeling it versus having it buried in one's heart to where it is making a significant difference. I have heard (and taught) if one knows God loves him, confidence is possible. That is not truly what brings about inner strength. Knowing intellectually he loves us helps, yes. Major difference comes when we can utterly rest in that. Put all our faith in that. Be at peace.

We can know God loves us and still worry. It is not because we do not believe in his love, but because we are not willing or able to stop worrying. I can know God loves me and still question my worth. If his love is defined as and limited to pity in my mind, and not as a passion for his daughter, its effect is less than life changing.

His love for me as his creation is immense and unconditional. I know this! Now it is my responsibility to move on and learn to embrace this newfound understanding of unfailing love from the Heavenly Father.

1-26

In light of all that has taken place, I think I am beginning to see that trust is not black and white, is not all or nothing, and it is okay to trust just a little bit. To stay at that spot and not take the next tiny step is to lock myself into solitary confinement. It is a good idea to learn to trust people who are offering affirmations, to begin challenging the belief that no good moment is deserved.

There is much work yet to do but with a new set of goals. Until now, I just wanted to function and manage mostly out of duty. Today I am excited. For the first time I see the possibility of one of those "happiest days of my life" actually happening.

Someday.

What a long road lies ahead! Old goals included I wanted people to hear my silent screams; now I am more interested in the scream becoming an audible, gentle appeal for the help I need. Once too tired to go on, I am willing to apply lessons learned to see how far they will take me. One goal was for peace to come to me, now I want to learn how to choose it for myself.

2-4

"It's different this time," Jerry insists with tears on his cheeks. "This time I am not just following rules, my heart is truly changing."

My eyes watch his with uncertainty.

"Nancy," he pleads. "Look at what is happening now. What we have never seen before in our marriage. I am in counseling and have recognized my powerlessness to conquer anything without God. Think how different marriage counseling is now compared to one year ago. I'm accepting responsibility, making decisions without blaming you. I am learning not to accuse you for what goes wrong in my life."

How can I go around this cycle again? How? We have been getting along generally well. Our love for each other has been declared in private and in public. It is trust that is missing. The next link needed in the chain.

This conversation piles on the already overwhelming emotions that have been creeping up in the last day or two. So many changes rushing at me in such a short period. Teaching those classes, striving to write for hours per day, entertaining new friends, receiving multiple emails from new acquaintances, dinner invitations, new members at the Depression Support Group, epiphanies, extreme fluctuating moods, trying to trust, attempting to improve...it's too much. Not all the necessary changes in my mind and heart can be expected to occur at once! One step. One notch.

So what is one thing I can do today to help my marriage?

Tomorrow, sometime tomorrow I will think more on Jerry's words. Crawling back into bed to hide under the covers is probably not the solution today. Nevertheless, it is what I choose to do.

2-6

Forget the former things; do not dwell on the past. See, I am doing a new thing! Now it springs up; do you not perceive it?

I am making a way in the desert and streams in the wasteland. The wild animals honor me, the jackals and the owls, because I provide water in the desert and streams in the wasteland, to give drink to my people, my chosen, the people I formed for myself that they may proclaim my praise.[5]

This Bible passage is about refocusing. A CBT verse. I am figuratively still in the desert at the time of this promise. Nowhere does it say God whisked me to an upscale resort where the springs are surrounded by palm trees and hired personnel are waiting on my every wish. No, the scene remains the desert where it is hot, dry, and nothing of a more comfortable situation can be spotted. This is where God is doing his new thing. In the wilderness. In the middle of my pain and struggle.

His springs are there, so do I perceive them? Or are my eyes focused on the sand? The streams in the wasteland are flowing; will I drink from them and praise God as the simple beasts do? On the other hand, am I smarter than that, more realistic, cynical?

Where will I place my eyes?

The past will not be forgotten. This scripture is a reminder to not keep score, or maintain a record. It is not a command to forget. History has to be remembered if I am to learn from it and grow. It is also a resource for learning to be safe in healthy ways. The child who has learned that abuse is unpredictable and often mixed with expressions of love, needs to recall the consequences in order to exercise good judgment with people who would mistreat her. To forget is to remain a walking target.

Still, her eyes can be on the waters offered by the Heavenly Father whose love is never a violation. Her spirit's refreshing can come from the source of life himself, while she remains in the desert of disappointment that sometimes others do not love her as they ought.

CBT, and scripture, are not about denying the negative aspects of life. Humanity will deal with thoughts, desires, feelings, and even behaviors we sense do not reflect God's best intentions for us. Acknowledging the existence of these negatives opens us to the question, "Do I want to stay in this spot, in this attitude? Or do I want to exercise a different sort of reaction to life's stressors?" It is then, not always easily but ever possible, we can refocus, look at the fresh water springing up around our situation and in our hearts.

Pollyanna does not live in this reality. She is too busy diving into the mirage of that fancy resort. Every time, she will hit sand. Our vision is not mirage.

God's promises are reality. The water is present. "See, I am doing a new thing...Do you not perceive it?"

2-8

Life is full of struggles. One year ago, I was barely breathing. A heavy shroud had been steadily draping itself over my shoulders and head a little more each day. As the world appeared increasingly gray and fuzzy, I was losing the capacity to maneuver in the diminishing light, to inhale under the dense blackness. Feeling a slab in the cold darkness, I laid down to rest, and closed my eyes.

The end to suffering was my goal, yet it was that undesired pain, confusion, and despair that ultimately opened the way to insight into my heart, mind, and past. This insight holds promise. Being able to identify truth is the first step of many to come that lead away from spiritual and emotional flatlining, and toward life. Understanding all this may be beyond my grasp, nonetheless there is one fact I do know; that for me, it took dying to survive.

As this journal evolved into a book, the symbolism of ending this story on January 15 appealed to my sense of artistic drama. That date came and went, yet the tale was not winding down. Weeks later it remains at full tilt; the end was not the end.

Life simply cannot be confined in a neat, little package. It is raggedy with pointy corners and does not gift-wrap easily. Instead of a happy sunset closing, reality's story calls for a different sort of conclusion.

When I was nine, a chicken named Peeper had become my little pet. One of twelve chicks intended for future dinners, Peeper was the smallest, the runt. At first, the tiny yellow balls of fuzz were confined to hopping around in a box in our basement, warmed by a lamp.

Larger chicks often bullied and held Peeper back. Since I was feeding her away from them, she began to grow. Fearing it could soon be difficult to recognize her apart from the others; I took a purple marker and colored a spot underneath one wing.

Shortly, a coop, actually a fence around an old shed in the backyard, received its eager residents. Hours later, our family returned from going out to dinner. The first thing I wanted to do was check on the chickens. Jumping out of the car and rounding the corner of the house, I stopped and stared. There was no fence. Chicken wire lay mangled near deep holes dug into the dirt. There were no chickens. Feathers shrouded the surrounding grass. A neighborhood dog had raided our coop.

Mournfully and in shock at the sight, I sat down on an old log in the deathly quiet, sick at heart.

"Cheep."

"It's not possible!" Springing to my feet, I looked around. There was no movement among the feathers. The shed, which had served briefly as their shelter, was empty. Nothing was hiding under the trees or in the tall weeds at the base of their trunks.

"Cheep."

It seemed to be coming from inside the dark shed. Taking a more careful look deep in the shadows, my eyes finally focused on a shape. A brick was leaning vertically against one wall.

"Cheep."

Flinging it aside, I see her—the one lone survivor. I knew my next hope was beyond reason. Carrying her to the sunlight, I held my breath while lifting one wing.

A purple mark.

Even my childish heart saw the irony. If Peeper had been bigger, she never would have fit behind that brick, never would have escaped the menacing jaws of some old dog. Her limitation saved her, and I in turn was blessed with a fun pet, and a great tale.

Life is full of struggles. Battles for the mind, for marriages, for health, for our children—these never end. Sometimes we grow weary, and want to quit. Those who keep walking despite how they feel may be encouraged by their progress, only to see it disappear under yet another wave of pain. Reality is life does that sometimes.

Might there be a purpose in all this?

Although it may seem mental illness limits my effectiveness, it can be the very channel through which my voice makes a difference. It is time to come out from behind the brick and try. Perhaps my resurrection can result in people being awed by God as it was with Lazarus. A few weeks before my suicide attempt, I heard on the radio the following: "Do not be afraid of your weakness, for it is the stage on which God's power and grace shine most bright." [6] Maybe God wants my life to demonstrate to other fragile souls how that works.

It is a challenge I now accept.

Appendix

For more information on Major Depression and suicide, see:

- http://www.nimh.nih.gov
- http://www.nami.org
- feelingblue.org

If you are in emotional distress or thinking about suicide, call the National Suicide Hotline at 1-800-273-TALK

If you are suicidal now with a plan, call 911 or go the nearest Emergency Room. There is hope!